SUTTON POCKET HISTORIES

THE EUROPEAN REFORMATION

VIVIAN GREEN

SUTTON PUBLISHING

First published in the United Kingdom in 1998 by
Sutton Publishing Limited · Phoenix Mill
Thrupp · Stroud · Gloucestershire · GL5 2BU

British Library Cataloguing in Publication Data
A catalogue record for this book is available from the British
Library.

ISBN 0-7509-1915-9

Cover illustration: Edward VI and the Pope by unknown artist
(courtesy National Portrait Gallery, London)

 ALAN SUTTON™ and SUTTON™ are the
trade marks of Sutton Publishing Limited

Typeset in 11/14.5 pt Baskerville.
Typesetting and origination by
Sutton Publishing Limited.
Printed in Great Britain by
The Guernsey Press Company Limited,
Guernsey, Channel Islands.

For William, to whom I owe so much

Contents

List of Dates

1530	The Augsburg Confession.
1531	Zwingli killed at the Battle of Kappel.
	Henry VIII recognized as supreme head of the English Church.
1533	Thomas Cranmer appointed Archbishop of Canterbury.
1534	Act of Supremacy.
1534	Fisher and More executed.
	Jesuits first formed (confirmed by the Pope, 1540).
1534–5	Anabaptists rule Münster.
1536	Calvin publishes *The Institutes of the Christian Religion*; goes first to Geneva.
	Dissolution of monasteries starts in England.
1541–64	Calvin chief pastor in Geneva.
1545	First meeting of the Council of Trent (reassembled 1551–2, 1562–3).
1546	Luther dies.
1547–53	Edward VI English king: Reformation strengthened.
1549	The First Book of Common Prayer.
	By the Consensus Tigurinus Swiss Protestants adopt Calvinism.
1552	Second Book of Common Prayer.
1553	Servetus executed at Geneva.
1553–8	Mary Tudor queen: Catholic reaction in England Latimer, Ridley and Cranmer burned.
1555	The Religious Peace of Augsburg recognizes Lutherans.
1559	John Knox begins the Reformation in Scotland.

ONE

The Medieval Background

The European Reformation swept like a religious hurricane through much of western Europe, making an immense impact upon religious life and belief and changing social and political conventions. No movement since the early days of Christianity was to be so widespread and so profound or so long-lasting in its effects. While it was not a revolution that challenged the basic supernatural interpretation of the universe nor the fundamental doctrines of Christianity, it was to wash away many familiar landmarks and to put new ones in their place. In some respects the religious face of western Christendom underwent a cosmetic reconstruction, for the old and established forms of worship and belief were to be overturned, the image of the past was to be shed as the winds of reform battered at the old buildings.

Yet the Reformation was as much an evolutionary process as a revolution, a movement emerging out

1

of the matrix of medieval Catholicism. Past historians have sometimes suggested that the Reformation was a response to the failings of the contemporary Church, more especially in its higher echelons. The late medieval Church was not, however, the sink of corruption and superstition that some Protestant apologists made it out to be. That there were some scandalous abuses cannot be denied. The Papacy had become unduly politicized, appearing as an overweight bureaucracy, an outwardly worldly institution located in a rich and luxurious court. After the unity of the Church had been restored by the Council of Constance following the Great Schism (1378–1415), when the Church had been divided by two men (and for a short while by three) competing for the papal tiara, the popes had been under the necessity of restoring their authority and strengthening their finances, at times to the loss of their spiritual reputation.

By a similar criterion many prelates were also found wanting, while many monasteries seemed no longer characterized by a deep concern for spirituality and the renunciation of the world that had once been their primary objective; but it was possible to point to monasteries and convents which did continue to be houses of prayer, scholarship and charity. The friars seemed to have lost their evangelical enthusiasm but in reformed orders like the Observant Franciscans there were signs of revived ardour.

There was some anti-clericalism in the sense that there were criticisms of the clerical order and its demands, especially Church dues such as tithes, but this had been an endemic feature of Christian history for many centuries. There is no particular reason to think that it was a stronger force in the late fifteenth century than it had been in earlier times, though it could, given the right circumstances, fester into violence.

The late medieval Church was in many respects a healthy and effective institution regarded with esteem by the majority of its members. Churches, great and small, continued to be built or rebuilt throughout Christendom. The faithful declared their allegiance by their gifts and in their wills. For most people the Church was the necessary gateway to salvation, the highway to that eternal life which none doubted. All recognized that they were sinners who were obliged to confess their sins at least once a year to a priest who would administer the sacrament of penance, giving them absolution conferring grace. They were obliged to attend the Mass, celebrated by a priest, recalling and in a sense re-enacting the offering which Christ made once and for all time on the Cross, the bread and wine physically transformed at the moment of consecration into Christ's body and blood. Whatever demands there might be for a reform of the Church's organization, the Church remained for most people the key to eternity, to the promise of Paradise, the road to Purgatory and conceivably the signpost to the fires of Hell. This was the system of belief which was in many ways to be overthrown by the Reformation.

However, there were some features in the late medieval world that, with hindsight, seemed to portend a measure of change. The great Church council meeting by the placid waters of Lake Constance had reconciled the Church and condemned heresy in the persons of John Wyclif and Jan Hus, but it had achieved nothing in the way of much-needed reform. Yet it had made one significant dent in the papal armoury by passing a decree (*Sacrosancta* in 1415) which declared that the authority of a general council was superior to that of the Pope. The Pope abrogated the decree and henceforth was wary of any demand for a general council but the point had been made.

In other ways, papal power underwent some constriction in the late Middle Ages. The authority of the heads of national states, as well as a sense of national identity itself, had greatly grown. The Pope's need to secure the backing of secular princes for the reanimation of his own authority and finances led to his making a series of agreements or concordats with the heads of states in Spain, France and the Empire, by which they secured greater influence over the Church in their states. It was a partnership that was of benefit to both sides but it underlined the extent to which the Pope depended ultimately on the support of lay sovereigns.

There was another aspect of the situation that had some bearing on the future in the shape of reform movements within the Church itself. There were some individual prelates who promoted reform in their own dioceses, seeking to improve the standard of clerical behaviour. Some monastic orders sought to restore something of the pristine way of monastic life. Perhaps of more positive importance was the fresh stimulus given to lay devotion, what was known as the *devotio moderna*. Lay men and women formed

communities like that of the Brethren of the
Common Life in the Low Countries, which, like
others, was designed to promote a better understanding of what constituted spirituality by encouraging those involved not merely to live a deeply
moral life, but also to believe that their digesting of
words of Scripture was a pathway to the ultimate
Vision of God. It was significant that the most
distinguished member of the Brethren of Common
Life was Thomas à Kempis, whose book *The Imitation
of Christ* was to become a handbook to the practice
of their religion for innumerable Catholics and
Protestants. Even more individualistic was mystical
theology by which, through contemplation and
prayer, the aspirant sought to achieve direct access
to God. Such men and women at all times formed a
small spiritual élite but they were influential; Luther,
for instance, owed much to the *Theologica Germanica*
and the German mystic John Tauler. Such
movements seemed in one sense to be trying to
bypass the sacramental system of the Church, in
order to secure a more intimate awareness of God.

There had been two unequivocal challenges to the
authority of the Church in the late Middle Ages – by
the Lollards in England and by the Hussites in

Bohemia. Heresy had been a recurrent feature of Church history. In the late twelfth and early thirteenth centuries the Albigensian or Cathar heresy had flourished in the south of France but had been eventually eliminated by persecution and preaching. Another group, the Waldensians, continued to exist in the Alpine valleys of northern Italy, in southern Italy and in Provence; their views, carried by travelling preachers, were heterodox but their communities were small and had only a minimal influence outside the area where they flourished.

Both Lollardy and Hussitism, the creation of University teachers, the Yorkshireman John Wyclif in England and Jan Hus in Bohemia, did not merely call for a more rigid application of Christian principle and the elimination of corruption but made an outright criticism of the nature of the Church itself and some of its fundamental doctrines, including the basic theory of the Mass, questioning the doctrine of transubstantiation. As he grew older, Wyclif became the more extreme in his views, vilifying the papal headship, attacking the ecclesiastical hierarchy, the monastic orders and the worship of saints. He maintained that Scripture interpreted in a literal sense should be the sole criterion for Christian belief and action, and he and his associates actually translated the Bible into English, a new and momentous step that alarmed the ecclesiastical authorities. Wyclif in England, as Jan Hus in Bohemia, attracted a popular following and even acquired some friends among the nobility, their criticism of the Church somehow coinciding with its lay supporters' political aims.

Wyclif died in his bed at Lutterworth in 1384 and after a period of prosecution and persecution the Lollards' following diminished, though it did not completely die out. Hus was sentenced to death but his followers became deeply entrenched as a political as well as a religious movement in Bohemia, albeit weakened by divisions in their own ranks. What was perhaps significant was that the Church could only effectively eliminate the enemy within by relying on the secular power, persuaded that any attack on the Church subverted its own authority. It raised the question as to what might happen if the secular authority instead of supporting the Church gave its hand to its critics. Although there was a tenuous link between Lollardy and the beginnings of the Reformation in England and between the Hussites and the spread of Lutheranism in central Europe, neither Lollardy nor Hussitism could be seen as a major ingredient, let alone a main cause, of the onset of the Protestant Reformation.

What else was there in the current situation that might be said to have favoured the growth of a movement such as the Reformation? No movement can develop in a social vacuum, so there must have been features in the general situation that helped to produce the seed-bed in which the movement took root.

The fifteenth century had seen some important intellectual developments, notably the emergence of humanism. The intellectual vitality of medieval Christendom had become concentrated in a body of learning described as scholasticism, whose greatest proponent was the thirteenth-century Dominican friar Thomas Aquinas. Aquinas, the author of the magnum opus *Theologica Scholastica*, had managed by a mastery of dialectic argument to marry ancient Greek, notably Aristotelian, philosophy with the dogmatic and theological teachings of the Church. But his philosophy, described generally as realism, had been questioned by a Franciscan thinker, Duns Scotus, who queried, reasonably enough, whether reason could in fact be used effectively to prove the truths of revelation, the validity of which depended, as he argued, ultimately on the faith of the believer.

Both the realists and the nominalists, as the followers of Scotus were known, had a following in the medieval universities. Indeed, the Nominalist emphasis on faith as the gateway to salvation and the stress on the absolute omnipotence of the Creator were to be taken over by Luther and the other Reformers. But the scholastics' concern with logic-chopping, their concentration on the minimalist points of theology, illustrated by the well-known debate as to how many angels could stand on top of a pin, seemed to many increasingly sterile. This was more especially the experience of scholars and thinkers attracted by the deeper accessibility of Greek philosophical thought, particularly that facilitated by the arrival of Greek scholars in Italy fleeing from the Turkish onslaught on the Byzantine empire.

The study of the ancient classics could lead at one extreme to a flirtation with neo-paganism but more generally it brought about a growing distaste for the intellectual aridities of scholasticism and a desire to read the Church Fathers and the Scriptures in their original tongues, so opening up a series of new vistas that subjected the Church and some of its teachings to a microscopic examination and critical scrutiny. Humanism was important in supplying some of the tools that the reformers would use.

In this intellectual renaissance no one was to play a more prominent part than the Dutch scholar Erasmus of Rotterdam, a former monk (eventually dispensed from his vows). Educated by the Brothers of the Common Life at Deventer, he was a scholar of international renown who took advantage of the newly invented printing press to publicize his views. He was concerned to edit the writings of the Fathers of the Church and, even more importantly, to prepare an edition of the New Testament based on the original sources. Published in 1516, the volume was imperfect but it took up the gauntlet where Wyclif had laid it down, opening a treasure chest from which the early Protestant reformers were to draw their material. Erasmus was also a satirist who held up to ridicule much contemporary religious practice and belief, such as the worship of relics (as in his *Praise of Folly*). Erasmus envisaged a restoration (*restitutio*) of Christianity but he was never a Protestant and died in 1536 a Catholic, buried in the minster at Basle. Nevertheless, in some sense he could be called the midwife of the Reformation.

Even more importantly, social changes were taking place which made it the more likely that a call to Reformation would find a response. The invention of the printing press was integral to its success. The movable-type printing press was not a cause of the Reformation but its availability was a necessary pre-condition to its successful outcome. That so many pamphlets were circulated throughout Europe at such an early date testifies to a substantial rise in literacy, as the foundation of so many universities and grammar schools in the fifteenth century would also suggest. Here was a reading public ready to lap up religious propaganda.

While late medieval Europe was still basically rural in its complexion, there were, especially in Germany, Italy and the Low Countries, bustling cities enriched by trade and banking. The early merchant capitalists were often hostile to the influence exerted by the local clergy over town life, and envious of their wealth. These cities, small as they seem to us now, housed a proletariat, workers and apprentices, an effervescent group who might readily respond to a call for mob violence. The social scene, affected in some areas by economic depression, was awash with tendencies that might promote religious change.

This was the scenario of the late medieval world. The stage was set but there were, as yet, no leading actors. If the tinder was dry, it required a spark to set it alight. The Reformation was not the work of any one man, but it had leaders who helped to fashion the ideas that gave it life. In its future craftsmen, Luther, Zwingli and Calvin, the Reformation found the men who could do this, the generals who provided the strategy, transmitted the enthusiasm and gave the lead to their waiting troops. The Reformation was never a wholly populist movement for, like other major revolutions, it was engineered in the first instance by comparatively few men and women, a zealous minority who by preaching and persuasion, and sometimes by threats of violence, secured a hearing and brought in the uncommitted. Often burdened by Church dues and unimpressed by their pastors, they listened readily to preachers who would provide a 'new look' on life, scripturally based, with an inbuilt promise of hope for this life and the life hereafter. The winds were soon to blow and become a gale that in many countries would overturn the existing structure of the Church and re-mould its teaching, affecting the social and political order.

TWO

Martin Luther & the German Reformation

Hans Luther had hoped that his son, Martin, would become a lawyer. Of peasant ancestry, Hans had done well for himself, becoming an affluent copperminer at Eisleben in Saxony. Martin was evidently an intelligent boy, for after schooling at Mansfield and Magdeburg at the age of eighteen he entered the University of Erfurt. To his father's dismay he was not to become a lawyer but the architect of a religious revolution. Like St Paul on the Damascus road he apparently had a semi-mystical experience that changed the direction of his life. Overtaken by a fierce thunderstorm, in fear for his life, 'terrore et agone mortis subitae circumvallatus', he prayed to St Anne, the patron saint of miners, promising her that if he emerged safe and sound he would dedicate his life to God as a monk.

Whatever the truth of this story, Martin Luther certainly abandoned the idea of becoming a lawyer and entered the order of the Augustinian Friars, an order that had recently experienced a measure of reform. But for all the austerity of the monastic life Luther lacked the reassurance of salvation, which he had hoped his renunciation of the world would bring him. 'The more I sweated it out, the less of peace and quiet I experienced.'

But while he was sweating it out as a friar, he had not neglected his academic studies, and was so promising a scholar that he was asked to lecture at the neighbouring University of Wittenberg, which had been founded recently by the local ruler, the Elector Frederick of Saxony. In the lectures that Luther gave to the students on the Pauline Epistles, glimmerings of his later theology could be glimpsed. He had come to the conclusion that salvation was less a matter of how one behaved, the works that one did, than what one believed, one's faith. The Church taught that salvation was granted by God to those who served Him with good works and unquestioning faith through the acceptance of the sacraments, of which the Church had the monopoly. Luther, however, believed that alone man was powerless to earn his salvation. Before the unutterable majesty of God, man must for ever remain imperfect, for ever a fallen creature. It was faith alone that 'justified' (God gives grace, not because we deserve it, but because He wishes to). Tortured by a sense of his own insufficiency, in a state of depression and spiritual shock, the message came upon Luther as a revelation of God's purpose. This notion of what came to be called 'justification by faith' could be traced back, through the writings of the early Christian fathers and St Augustine in particular, to St Paul but it was Luther who was to highlight it and make it the core of his message. By applying the litmus test of Scripture, Luther was in effect to dismantle much of the belief and practice of the Roman Church.

Whether or not this burning belief burst upon Luther like a flash of light in a dark corner, the actual process of adapting his mind to this new-found interpretation of true religion was to be slow and painful. One landmark occurred on the eve of All Saints' Day 1517, when he addressed ninety-five theses of protest denouncing indulgences to the Archbishop of Mainz, which he may then conceivably but not certainly have affixed to the door of the Castle Church at Wittenberg. An indulgence was theologically a pardon, offered in return for payments (and in theory conditional on the efficacy of the contrition shown by the sinner). In this case, the proceeds were to go to the rebuilding of St Peter's basilica at Rome, as well as towards repayment of the debts that the Elector Archbishop Albert of Mainz, who had approved the indulgence, owed to the bankers Fuggers of Augsburg. The indulgence seller was a Dominican friar, John Teztel, who was about to enter Saxony. The Elector Frederick resented his incursion in his territory, fearing the influence of his cousin and rival, Duke George. Luther's opposition was theological. He rejected as a hideous blasphemy the concept that pardon for sin could be bought, a notion that cut across his whole understanding of the true nature of forgiveness which was given freely by Christ through the faith of the believer. 'As the penny in the coffer rings, the soul from Purgatory springs.'

Once Luther had made this protest, he had, as it were, opened the floodgates. The Dominican friars, rivals of the Augustinians, reported the matter to Rome. Luther was summoned there to explain himself – he had earlier visited Rome as a pilgrim – but, supported by the Elector Frederick, he made excuses. Next year, in October 1518, provided with a safe conduct, he engaged in an abortive debate with the

Thomist scholar, the papal legate Cardinal Cajetan, at Augsburg. In another debate, in June 1519, with the wily and learned theologian John Eck at Leipzig, he was led on to express his sympathy with Jan Hus and to declare that a general council's authority was greater than that of a pope. This was dangerous ground.

What was astonishing was the speed with which Luther's critical views began to circulate, not merely in Germany but well beyond its borders and in the main through the medium of the printing press. Three important pamphlets came from his pen in 1520: *To the Christian Nobility of the German Nation*, a virulent attack on the Papacy, in which he called on the German princes to take the lead in reforming the Church; the *Babylonish Captivity of the Church*, in which he criticized the sacramental teaching of the Church; and *Of the Liberty of a Christian Man*, in which he declared that there were only three sacraments, baptism, penance and the Eucharist, and extolled the doctrine of justification by faith, 'for faith alone, and the efficaciousness of the Word of God, bring salvation'. The Pope, he had written, is a 'man of sin and the son of perdition who sits in the Church like God and by his doctrines and statutes increases the sin of the Church and the destruction of souls'.

Even the genial sybaritic Pope Leo X was stirred into action; on 15 June 1520, from his hunting lodge where he was chasing wild boar, he issued a papal bull – *Exsurge Domine* – in which some forty-one of Luther's tenets were condemned as heretical. In a show of defiance, Friar Martin, never a conciliatory man, flung the papal bull together with the books of the canon law into a bonfire at Wittenberg, declaring that 'You have condemned the truth of God. He also condemns you to the fire.'

The papal bull had been published throughout Germany, and Luther had now to deal with the reaction of his political superior, the Emperor Charles V, a callow 21-year-old Fleming who was also the King of Spain. Germany was an amorphous collection of semi-independent states and cities over which the Emperor, whose own territories were confined to Austria, held nominal sway. Charles was a loyal Catholic, much disgusted by what had been reported about this insolent friar, commenting that 'a single friar who goes counter to all Christianity for a thousand years must be wrong'.

Luther was summoned to attend a meeting of the Imperial Diet, set to meet at Worms in April 1521 and over which the Emperor presided. He was promised a safe conduct but he was uneasily aware that this had not saved Jan Hus from the stake over a century earlier. Nervous as he was, he stood his ground: 'truly with the help of Christ I will not reverse even an iota into all eternity. Here I stand, God help me, I can do no other.' The attempt to refute Luther and make him repent had evidently failed. The Emperor would have no alternative but to condemn him as a 'notorious heretic'. Luther and his companions swiftly left the city, doubtless fearful but still alive, an outcome which in later life the Emperor deplored as a fatal mistake.

The immediate sequel was strange but ultimately providential. Luther's patron, the Elector Frederick, who much esteemed his services at his cherished University of Wittenberg, eager to ensure his safety, had him kidnapped and placed in detention at the Wartburg Castle where he grew a beard and was known as 'Junker Georg'.

In his enforced isolation, Luther experienced constipation, a habitual complaint, and severe bouts of depression that may well have been aggravated by feverish nightmares, in which he dreamed that the Devil was trying to get him into his clutches. But as a counter to this morbidity, he was engaged in a task of epochal importance, the translation of the New Testament into German, completed by the end of February 1522; the Old Testament was slowly to follow, finally published in 1534.

Luther was brought back into the world by news from Wittenberg, where his friend and follower, the ardent Carlstadt, had organized a radical religious revolution. He and his rampaging followers had cast out the recalcitrant priests, overturned the altars and images, closed the monasteries, ordered the Communion to be distributed in both kinds (hitherto only the bread had been given to the communicants) and confiscated religious funds that were put to the relief of the poor. Luther welcomed the changes but was worried by the violence, as was the Elector of Saxony; 'the common man', the Elector said sternly, 'has been incited to folly'. So Luther returned to Wittenberg and, supported by his friend the scholarly moderate Philip Melanchthon, took the situation in hand. The changes were not reversed but in reorganizing the new Church, for that was what it was, the procedure began to be more orderly.

Basically there was a strong element of conservatism in Luther's religious and political ideas. Like most of his contemporaries, Luther believed that the social order was God-given, constituting a chain of being that permeated the universe as well as the world, any disturbance of which was likely to be inspired by the Devil. He was not looking ahead to the future. He did not suppose that he was founding a new Church. He was seeking to restore what he fondly believed to be the early Christian community, that historical fiction which has bewitched so many would-be reformers.

This concern for order was soon revealed in Luther's attitude to a violent social upheaval, the Peasants' War of 1524–5, an inchoate movement of protest by the peasants of south Germany, in Thuringia and Saxony, brought about by their wish to protect their ancient rights and privileges that were threatened by new demands from their landlords. Led eventually by a charismatic religious enthusiast, Thomas Müntzer, who described Luther as 'Dr Pussyfoot, the new pope of Wittenberg', it was very violent; some seventy monasteries were said to have been sacked in Thuringia and fifty-two in Franconia.

Perhaps fearful that his religious teaching might in part be thought responsible, Luther reacted strongly. In a furiously worded pamphlet, *Against the Thievish and Murderous Hordes of Peasants*, he urged the forces of law and order led by the princes 'to smite, slay and stab'; 'if the peasant is in open rebellion then he is outside the law of God, for rebellion is not simply murder, but it is like a great fire which attacks and lays waste a whole land.' The peasants suffered a mortal defeat at Frankenhausen in May 1525.

In effect, the Lutheran Reformation was being politicized. Who was responsible for introducing and safeguarding the religious changes that Luther and his followers prescribed? Whatever Luther wrote about the 'priesthood of believers', it was not the congregation but the godly prince who made it possible. Luther himself had had the inestimable benefit of the support of the Elector Frederick the Wise of Saxony and, to a greater extent, of his more distinctively Protestant brother and successor, the Elector John Frederick. If there was no godly prince, then the way was open for the chaos of war and upheaval. Luther was no democrat nor indeed in the circumstances of his time could he have been. In the upshot, the progress of the Reformation in Germany depended upon the support that it received from the powers in charge, whether churchmen, city magistrates or princes.

But the Reformation did not lack popular support. At the time of the Diet of Worms the papal legate Cardinal Aleander had gloomily reported that nine-tenths of Germany supported Luther. While this may have been an overstatement, the rapid spread of the Reformation in German lands was undeniable. What were the forces that brought this about? Martin Luther stayed at Wittenberg, which soon became a centre of pilgrimage for German and foreign scholars; Shakespeare would have us believe that Hamlet, Prince of Denmark, was among them.

Otherwise, for most Germans, Luther himself must have been a very remote figure, known personally only to few of his followers, glimpsed in some engravings and woodcuts, but for the most part a voice broadcast through the travelling preachers, often former monks, and the multitudinous pamphlets that poured forth from the printing presses. It was the message rather than the man that attracted a following. It must not be forgotten that fundamentally the Reformation was a religious movement with a message that seemed to fill a spiritual vacuum. The Lutherans were to find in their congregations a fellowship and a liturgy in their own language, together with a home life often enriched by prayer and hymns, of which Luther himself was a masterly composer, and the reading of the German Bible. It is utterly impossible to recover the thrill and sense of wonder that some of these sixteenth-century men and women felt as they read in their own language the stories of the Old Testament prophets and of the teaching, life and sayings of Jesus. While the Bible often seems perhaps unreadable or incomprehensible to many twentieth-century men and women, to some of our European ancestors at least the opportunity to read the Bible seemed like opening a door into a secret garden of heavenly delight, of which they had been too long deprived. The reader might well have felt spiritually revived, a new man or woman assured in a way that he or she had never been before, that he or she was now reborn, saved through faith in the sacrifice that Christ had made on the Cross and the forgiveness that he consequently offered to the true believer for his or her sins and shortcomings.

Even so, this individual change of heart, which affected some princes, nobles, merchants and their wives, as well as some Catholic bishops, would not have brought the Reformation into being and to the apex of success if other primary factors had not been at work.

The Imperial cities in which the Reformation had its first successes were home to a population of affluent merchants, bankers and industrialists as well as a growing and increasingly literate middle class and a body of young apprentices and workers. Here too there tended to be a deep-rooted anticlericalism, often provoked by the privileges and power enjoyed by the local cathedral and clergy. Apart then from a favourable response to the reformed teaching, the citizens were to some extent moved by a desire to divest the clergy and the religious houses of the wealth and influence that they had long enjoyed while the young and impressionable could be easily stirred to riot and mayhem against the ecclesiastical establishment.

Martin Luther prided himself on being a German but in a strict sense there was no Germany, only an amorphous collection of semi-autonomous states under the nominal sovereignty of the Emperor. None the less, there was such a thing as German national feeling, which Luther from time to time invoked in his writings. During the fifteenth century German writers had unearthed ancient legends to praise the Germanic pastoral simplicity and martial valour; the *Nibelungenlied* played a similar part in promoting the German identity as the Arthurian legend did in contemporary England. Luther's attacks on the Papacy as an Italian institution battening on the pockets as well as the minds of the German people found a ready response.

The Reformation in Germany created a political divide that portended violence as the princes formed armed leagues to defend their interests. More immediately, there had been an uneasy peace that had allowed the Lutheran churches to organize themselves. The condemnation of Luther issued at the Diet of Worms in 1521 remained a dead letter. The Emperor Charles V had too many problems on his hands – as late as 1529 the Turks had besieged Vienna – and he was in any case convinced that in the interests of the Church the Pope should call a General Council to consider reforms, a step that the Pope was to be long reluctant to take. Moreover, there remained an influential middle party which still hoped that a compromise might be reached between the conflicting interests; in 1530 a Confession of Faith, largely composed by Melanchthon, had been drawn up at Augsburg that seemed momentarily to have some chance of success. So although two armed camps were being brought into being, a religious armistice for a time held sway.

Martin Luther stayed sedately at Wittenberg. The 'Wittenberg Nightingale', as Hans Sachs called him, continued to pour forth writings, still attacked the Pope and his other enemies with vigorous, even occasionally obscene, language but was equally capable of producing moving, devotional works. His marriage to the former nun Katherine von Bora, originally based on convenience rather than love, turned out to be exceptionally successful. He fathered a family, took in students who greedily wrote down what they remembered of his conversation, but as he grew older and his health declined, so his spirits burned low. His death from a heart attack at the age of sixty-three in 1546 marked the end of an epoch, though his creative work had been achieved so much earlier.

Before Luther died, violent war had broken out between the Protestant princes and the Imperial Catholic forces. A league of Protestant princes under the lead of Elector John Frederick of Saxony and Philip of Hesse had been concluded at Schmalkalden in 1531. Some sixteen years later, on 24 April 1547, the Catholic Emperor Charles V defeated the Schmalkaldic League, at the battle of Mühlberg, even taking the Protestant Saxon Elector a prisoner. But the Catholics were not really strong enough to force a solution. In 1548, in what might have seemed a sensible decision, the Emperor issued an *Interim*, allowing the people to follow the faith of their sovereign until, it was hoped, a General Council of the Church (which had actually met at Trent in 1545 but then was suspended) settled the issues at stake. In practice the *Interim* was to be overshadowed by the subsequent treaty of Passau in 1552, which anticipated what was for many years to be the pragmatic solution to the problem of a religiously divided Germany when in 1555 at Augsburg the principle of what was known as *cujus regio ejus religio* was established. Henceforth the prince was to determine the religion in his territory whether Lutheran or Catholic; there was no provision for the growing body of Calvinists. If the Emperor Charles V had spent over thirty years trying to stem the spread of Lutheranism, he had suffered a permanent defeat. Tired and disappointed, he withdrew from the political scene to pass his few remaining years in the quiet of the Spanish monastery of Yuste.

The Lutheran Reformation had come of age. In spite of future internal divisions, Lutheranism had acquired an abiding identity. Always aware of the prophetic presence of Martin Luther, it had become a Church that bore the hallmarks of his teaching and personality. Central to it was his notion of what constituted the Church, the *communio sanctorum,* the gathered community of all those who had accepted Christ as their saviour, in the last resort an invisible com-munity but represented on earth, if imperfectly, by the Christian congregation. Ideally Luther adumbrated the 'priesthood of all believers' – 'Let everyone who knows himself to be a Christian be assured that we are all priests.' But in the same way that he had come to accept the determinant authority of the godly prince, so for convenience and order there had to be those who served as ministers.

With the formation of churches, there came into existence a rich liturgy, conservative rather than radical in character. If the Word of God replaced the Mass as the centre-piece of the service, unlike his fellow reformer Zwingli, Luther still insisted that Christ was really present in the Eucharist, a theory known as consubstantiation, according to which while the materialistic changes were dismissed the Eucharist was more than a mere representation or memorial, signifying a spiritual change that could evoke a response from the worshipper. The real strength of Lutheranism lay in what may be described as its social cohesiveness, its schools and colleges where its ministers were well trained, its active concerns for helping the poor, needy and infirm.

Lutheranism was, then, the basis of German Protestantism, notwithstanding the fact that Calvinism was later to make its presence felt, as a powerful and persisting force in German life, providing a rich cultural heritage that was the medium through which a strong musical tradition, exemplified by the compositions of J.S. Bach, and a long-lasting theological scholarship were to be fashioned. The weakness of the Lutheran Church seemed to spring from its continued subordination to the authority of the state, which from time to time seemed to inject a measure of spiritual sterility and could lead to some odd situations, as in 1817 when the Prussian King Frederick-William III made a forced union of the Lutheran and Calvinist churches in his domain. Similarly the Nazis were to invoke the support of the Lutheran Church, not altogether without success; Luther's own anti-Semitic sentiments were recalled. Simultaneously it must be noted that Lutheranism occasionally gave rise to healthy dissent, as was shown by the repeated attempts of the Pietists in the late seventeenth and early eighteenth centuries to promote devotional life and spirituality, while in more recent times the Lutheran pastors Niemöller and Bonhoeffer were to be found in the vanguard of the opposition to Nazism.

Luther's teachings had soon crossed the frontiers of Germany. German merchants at the London steelyard brought them into England; Cardinal Wolsey ordered the burning of Lutheran literature. Archbishop Cranmer married the niece of a Lutheran pastor, Osiander, so breaching the vow of chastity, and was to absorb many of Luther's ideas, even if ultimately the English Reformation developed in a different direction. In France early reformers read and absorbed Luther's tracts and the reception of reformed ideas in the Low Countries seems very likely to have been Lutheran in origin.

It was, however, only in Scandinavia that Lutheranism outside Germany took permanent root. There were three impulses at work: the preaching of Lutheranism by evangelists, often trained at Wittenberg; the comparative decline of Roman Catholicism in these northern countries; and the self-interest of the kings and their nobles in promoting reform. In Denmark the leading exponent of Lutheranism was Hans Tausen, a peasant's son and a former monk who had studied at Wittenberg, returned to Jutland to preach the reformed teaching and, after imprisonment for so doing, had become chaplain to the Danish king, Frederick I. The National Assembly, meeting at Copenhagen in 1529, approved reform and drew up a Protestant Confession of Faith, the *Herredag*. Royal support that had won over the nobles against the powerful clergy secured the victory of Lutheranism, confirmed when the Augsburg Confession, the *Confessio Hefnica*, was accepted in 1530. Frederick I's successor, Christian III, took the Danish Reformation further, abolishing the office of bishop and reorganizing Church property.

Events in Sweden were to follow a similar pattern. At the beginning of the sixteenth century Sweden, Denmark, Norway, Finland and Iceland constituted a single federation under the Danish king but in the reign of the unbalanced Christian II of Denmark the union began to fragment as a Swedish noble, Gustavus Vasa, managed to restore his country's independence. To win the support of the nobility and to strengthen the Crown's impoverished finances Vasa decided to target the rich Swedish

Church. Lutheran preachers were soon at work; Olaus Petri, a blacksmith's son, who had studied at Wittenberg, was appointed royal chancellor and became the leading exponent of doctrinal change while his brother, Laurentius Petri, the first Protestant Archbishop of Upsala, translated the New Testament into Swedish. At a meeting of the Swedish Diet called by Vasa at Västerås in 1527 the Diet dissolved the monasteries and confiscated their properties to the benefit of the Crown and the nobility.

The future of the Reformation in Sweden was to be put at risk by a future king, John III, who tried in vain to bring about a compromise between the contending faiths, and by his son, Sigismund, a Roman Catholic. However, with the strong support of the nobility, who had a vested interest in the continuance of the Reformation, the Swedish Reformation was assured, so much so that in the following century, during the Thirty Years War, the Swedish King Gustavus Adolphus emerged as the principal champion of Protestantism against the Catholic powers.

THREE

Zwingli & the Swiss Reformation

The mountainous canton of Glarus in central Switzerland, populated by peasant farmers, may seem an unlikely birthplace for one of the more radically minded of the Protestant reformers, but there at Wildhaus in the Toggenburg on 1 January 1484, a few months before Luther's birth, Huldreich Zwingli was born. Taught Latin by his uncle, Bartholomew, Zwingli's higher education took him much further afield, to Basle, Berne, conceivably Paris, and then Vienna. Zwingli himself emerged with humanist sympathies, attracted by the writings of Erasmus and soaking himself in the works of the Greek fathers and St Augustine. He settled at Basle but such was his reputation that, although not yet ordained a priest, he was invited to become parish priest at Glarus where he celebrated his first Mass in his own parish church on 29 September 1506.

During the next few years he continued to read widely. He went as a pilgrim to Rome, which he liked no better than Luther, even though he was appointed a papal acolyte. More significantly he acted as chaplain to the Swiss mercenaries, the tough peasant soldiers ready to supplement their hard earnings by fighting for a paymaster, in this case the Milanese, who suffered a severe defeat at the hands of the French at Marignano in 1515. His experience made him doubly suspicious of foreigners and of the Italians in particular for he was at heart a Swiss patriot.

Switzerland was a group of semi-autonomous cantons joined together in a federation that had originally won independence from their Austrian overlords in August 1291. After serving as a chaplain, Zwingli moved as parish priest to Einsiedeln, a village a few miles north of the lake of Lucerne, the site of a well-known Benedictine abbey. He continued to read the New Testament, the Greek text of which had been published recently by Erasmus, reaching the conclusion that the life of the present Church compared unfavourably with the Church of the early centuries.

Then, in 1518, he applied for and was elected to the office of people's priest at the Grossmünster, the principal church at Zürich, the geographical location of which, at the head of a lake, had made it a centre of communication and thus one of the richest of the Swiss cantons, dominated by an aspiring merchant aristocracy. Zwingli's preaching attracted attention, partly because of his powers as an orator but even more so because of the extent to which his sermons were suffused by his Scriptural exegesis. 'The word of God', he declared, 'is certain and cannot fail; it is bright and does not let man err in the darkness; it recalls itself, it makes itself plain and illumines the human world with all salvation.' Some called him a follower of Luther but he denied the charge: 'I have not learnt the teaching of Christ from Luther but from the very word of God.'

His emphasis on the Scriptures appeared soon to have practical importance. When an indulgence seller, Bernard Samson, came to Zürich he was sent packing. Zwingli urged that the payment of tithes to the Church should be made voluntary and even abolished. His earlier life, as he confessed, had not been free from 'self-indulgence' but he had now married a young widow, Anna Reinhard, so breaking his vow of celibacy, an action he justified in his pamphlet *Archeteles* on scriptural grounds. His growing reputation advanced when he left Grossmünster to become the chaplain to the city council.

His new position placed him in a strong vantage point for introducing reform. In the next few years the city council authorized the abolition of the Mass, which Zwingli, more extreme than Luther, interpreted as a purely memorial celebration of the Last Supper. Monks and nuns were encouraged to leave their religious houses; in 1524 the abbess of the immensely wealthy Fraumünster handed over her house to the city council. Images, roods and crucifixes were taken down, relics were destroyed. At Zwingli's suggestion the city council used some of the resources from the confiscated religious property to help in the relief of the poor and to improve education.

Although Zwingli had won massive support, he was faced with some hostility and criticism from displaced priests and Catholics, among them merchant families. But not all the opposition came from the traditionalists. The inhabitants of some of the lakeside villages, Zolliken, Witikon and Höngg, and the richer community of Rapperswil at the eastern end of the lake, listened eagerly to more radical preachers. These were mainly Anabaptists, who taught that as infant baptism has no support in Scripture, adult baptism was an essential qualification for Church membership. Zwingli held that infant baptism was essential to membership of the Christian community and he was backed by the city council, which decreed that those who preached and practised to the contrary were liable to the death penalty. Consequently, an Anabaptist leader was drowned in the waters of the river Limmat.

More dangerous than the Anabaptists (who were none the less to be prescribed until 1798) was the growing opposition of the Catholic cantons, headed by Lucerne, together with Uri, Schwyz, Unterwalden and Zug, which met at the lakeside village of Beckenried to resist the spread of Protestant teaching.

In spite of this growing hostility, Protestantism in its Zwinglian form was crossing the steep Alpine passes and creeping up the mountain valleys. The former Dominican friar Sebastian Wagner or Hofmeister, converted by Zwingli, brought the northern town of Schaffhausen by the Rhine Falls to the reformed faith. The northern city of St Gallen, so long in tutelage to its rich abbey, greeted the reformed preachers. St Gallen's example was followed by the neighbouring canton of Appenzell and by Zwingli's own home county of Glarus and the Toggenburg. In eastern Switzerland Protestantism was to invade the loose federation of towns and mountain valleys known as the Grisons, nominally subject to the Bishop of Chur and open to Catholic influences from northern Italy. By the Articles of Ilanz, signed on 25 July 1526, much of the Grisons accepted the reformed faith, though the final picture was, as it has remained, a confused religious patchwork, the eastern-most valley, the Engadine, emerging strongly Protestant, its western neighbour remaining strongly Catholic.

In the centre of Switzerland lay the wealthy city of Berne, an Imperial city that was deeply opposed to the Emperor Charles V, virtually free from episcopal control and ruled by an aristocratic oligarchy. One of Zwingli's disciples, Berchtold Haller, had been appointed to a stall in the minster at Berne as early as 1520. Although the Small Council of Berne, dominated by the aristocrats, took no firm action, the Great Council, more representative of the merchants and artisans, grasped the opportunity offered by the acceptance of Protestantism to confiscate Church properties. With the arrival of other leading reformers, Bucer from Strasbourg, Oecolampadius from Basle and Zwingli from Zürich, the result at Berne was a foregone conclusion. By 1528 Berne, like Zürich, became a Protestant canton. Mercenary service abroad was forbidden. Unlike in Zürich, the proceeds of confiscated Church property seems not to have been put to any significant social or educational use.

In the north-west was the city of Basle, which had early attracted humanist writers, situated as it was virtually on the frontiers of the empire. At the end of 1522 a Hebrew scholar and preacher, John Hussgen of Weinsberg, who had assisted Erasmus with his translation of the New Testament, arrived in the city, taking the name Oecolampadius. He was in some sense a disciple of Zwingli, with whom he carried on a lively correspondence. The city council, strongly representative of mercantile interests, welcomed his message and was eventually persuaded to exile its bishop to Porrentruy. At first the city council had been ready to allow men and women to worship as they willed but by 1529 they insisted on the acceptance of Zwinglianism. With reluctance, Erasmus, who found this decision illiberal, left the city.

Within ten years, largely through the influence of Zwingli, sustained by Luther's writings, many of the leading Swiss cantons had been converted to the

Protestant faith. There was naturally a hostile reaction from the Catholic cantons, which, with the promised support of the Emperor's brother, Ferdinand of Austria, formed a Christian Union at Waldshut in April 1529. It brought pressure to bear on two other Swiss cantons, the Valais and Fribourg, to embrace the Catholic cause. One disciple of Zwingli's, a Züricher, was arrested by the Catholics while he was preaching the Gospel at Uznach (which, to complicate the issue, was under the joint or common jurisdiction of the Catholic canton of Schwyz and the Protestant canton of Glarus), and subsequently sentenced to be burned at the stake.

The Zürichers interpreted this as an act of war and, under Zwingli's lead, an armed band advanced on Zug but Berne intervened to restore peace by arranging a compromise by which the Catholic cantons agreed to renounce their alliance with Ferdinand of Austria and to permit freedom of worship in the common bailwicks. In the uneasy peace that followed, the German Protestant Prince Philip of Hesse, in an effort to strengthen the Protestant cause, decided that the time had come to seek to reconcile its two leading exponents, Luther and Zwingli, divided particularly by disagreement over the interpretation of the Eucharist.

Subsequently, in the early autumn of 1529, he arranged a meeting, which was attended by some other Protestant theologians, notably Bucer and Oecolampadius, at his castle at Marburg in southern Germany. The meeting was far from satisfactory. Luther was in no mood to compromise or even to discuss the issues. He simply wrote on the table in chalk 'Hoc est meum corpus', an expression of his conviction that Christ was truly present in the Eucharist, asserting that the bread and wine did not merely 'signify' the body and blood of Christ, but that Christ was 'ubiquitous', able to be present in the Mass, a view that Zwingli rejected. The conference ended with a bland report, simply rejecting the sacrificial interpretation of the Mass. Zwingli was back in Zürich by 19 October, reinforcing his understanding with his fellow Protestants in Basle and Strasbourg while the German princes, under the lead of Philip of Hesse, formed a common league against the Emperor and his Catholic supporters.

Relations between Zürich and the Catholic cantons were again deteriorating. The issues were as much political as religious. The Catholics complained that Zwingli was using unacceptable means to forward the Protestant cause in Thurgau. The Protestants asserted that the Catholics had broken the agreement made previously at Kappel to allow for freedom of worship in the common lands, that is the bailwicks under the joint jurisdiction of the two cantons. Zwingli, whose cause had become identified with his city's political ambitions, believed that his opponents could be brought to book by imposing an economic blockade. The Catholic cantons felt that they had no alternative except to resort to arms, declaring war on Zürich at Lucerne on 4 October 1531. The Zürichers were surprisingly ill-prepared. Zwingli led a motley band of volunteers only to be defeated at the Battle of Kappel on 11 October; Zwingli was himself among the slain.

The battle was a turning point, for it swept away Zwingli's hopes for a grandiose united Protestant Switzerland and confirmed Switzerland's religious as well as political diversity. Each canton was to determine its own form of faith while the status quo was maintained in the common lands. If Zürich lost no territory, its imperialistic ambitions had been brought to nought and even its economic as well as its political influence had been diminished.

Yet Zwingli's influence as a reformer cannot be gainsaid and his influence lived on. His religious successor (though not his political one) was

Heinrich Bullinger, a thoughtful humanist but a far less masterful personality. He remained a channel for the transmission of Zwingli's ideas, expanding and interpreting his teaching and engaging in an extensive correspondence with his fellow reformers, especially with English reforming circles during the reign of Edward VI.

Yet Zwinglianism, grafted as it was on to many Protestant systems and having had a vital part to play as a centre of an evangelical network in bringing about the Reformation in Switzerland, was too inchoate to provide a creed or even a Church of its own. It was inevitable that it should be ultimately absorbed into the more highly organized and more dogmatic system that sprang from another reformer of genius, John Calvin of Geneva. By the *Consensus Tigurinus* Zürich was to accept Calvin's teaching on the Sacraments. The Helvetic Confession was to determine that the Swiss Protestants would be Calvinistic in their organization and creed. Yet Zwingli remained one of the creative figures of the Reformation and the city with which he had identified himself a centre of reformed teaching.

FOUR

The English Reformation

Although in the course of its history England has
been occupied by the Romans, the Anglo-Saxons,
the Vikings and the Normans, and later governed
by Scottish, Dutch and German princes, its destiny
has been largely shaped by its insular character. It
is this fact that in many respects explains the
course of the English Reformation. The country
has never had a charismatic leader like Luther or
Calvin nor an outstanding popular evangelist. The
Protestants were a minority rather than a popular
movement, for it was not until the close of the
reign of Elizabeth I that England could be really
called a Protestant nation. The English
Reformation was largely initiated under the
auspices of the Crown and was sustained by the
established order, more especially the great noble
families who, in spite of their constant and deadly
rivalry, came to have a vested interest both in

gaining the favour and patronage of the Crown and in controlling the Church and its resources.

None the less, there were some developments that made so major a revolution feasible. The late medieval Church in England seems to have been in reasonably good fettle, governed by conscientious prelates often more learned in the intricacies of the law than the principles of theology and readily taking their lead from the Crown. The Church was served by a parochial clergy variable in the performance of their duties as they had ever been but in general esteemed by their flocks. There was some continuing anti-clericalism, but this would do no more than add a few coals to the fire when the fire was lit. There had indeed been some recurrence of Lollardy, which led the bishops to initiate a new series of heresy trials. If then there was a tentative connection between the flickering embers of Lollardy, especially in the Chilterns and the north of England, and the outbreak of the Reformation, it was not of crucial importance, affecting only a very small fraction of the population. Renaissance humanism had made some inroads into English academic and clerical life; the sermons of Dean Colet of St Paul's, for instance, stressed the Scriptural basis of the faith but it was to provide a tool for the reformers rather than to be a reason for reform. Lutheran literature trickled into the country, especially into London, but its influence was as yet limited. There seemed to be little in the situation that made the Reformation likely or suggested the direction that it would take. It was perhaps the comparatively slow and unpredictable course that the English Reformation took which caught the public unawares. The English Reformation was an indigenous movement, shaped by the natural course of events in which, for the most part, the majority of English people were obliged to acquiesce.

The spur, then, was not to be found in the activities of prophets and preachers but in the personal needs of the English king, Henry VIII. Henry VIII, still comparatively young, active, attractive and intelligent, as yet far from being the psychopathic monster that he ultimately became, was a self-centred man who did not brook any opposition to his royal will. He had some knowledge of theology, having helped to pen a tract in confutation of Martin Luther that earned him, ironically, the title of 'Defender of the Faith' from the Pope. Since 1509 he had been married to the Spanish Princess Catherine of Aragon, the widow of his brother Arthur, but she had produced only a daughter, Mary, and suffered a series of miscarriages, thus failing to give Henry the son and heir he so badly wanted. Her husband, highly sexed, though better in the chase than in its fulfilment, let his eye rove to other ladies, among them Mary Boleyn and her sister, the Lady Anne, with whom Henry had fallen desperately in love, if his love letters to her can be taken at their face value. Like most men and women of his age, Henry, for all his learning, was very superstitious. The man who later persuaded himself that Anne Boleyn had cast a spell on him had become convinced that the text in the Old Testament book Leviticus, which declared that a man who married his brother's wife had broken the law of God and was so accursed, sincerely came to the conclusion that his marriage to Catherine had been doomed because of his sin.

There was, however, much more than personal issues at stake. Henry's minister and confidant for many years was the able and arrogant Cardinal Wolsey, who greatly valued the Anglo-Spanish alliance as a pivot in English foreign policy. It happened that the King of Spain, who was also the Emperor Charles V, was Catherine's nephew. Charles had only recently sacked Rome and virtually taken the Pope, Clement VII, into captivity. The Emperor could not approve of Henry's attempt to rid himself of his aunt, and the Pope, however much he may have wished to issue a dispensation to annul the marriage, dared not take this step.

There followed a series of semi-farcical scenes, tinged by tragedy, which were designed to find a way out of the situation. Catherine denied that her marriage to Arthur had ever been consummated and appealed to Rome. The king began to lose patience, especially with Wolsey, whom death alone was to save from complete disgrace. Henry had, however, discovered new allies among Anne Boleyn's supporters, principally the Machiavellian figure of one of Wolsey's former servants, the able and ruthless Thomas Cromwell, who was drawn to the reformed teaching, and a churchman, Thomas Cranmer, whom the king had already employed on diplomatic missions to Spain and Rome, a Cambridge don whose own ideas were becoming more and more strongly laced by reformed teaching. The convenient death of the aged Archbishop of Canterbury, William Warham, paved the way for Cranmer's elevation to the see. He pronounced the marriage of Henry and Catherine at an end, while Henry married Anne. Whatever the views of the English people (and we know that there was some popular sympathy for Catherine) the English governing class and the English bishops had acquiesced in what had happened without of course realizing its long-term consequences.

Meanwhile measures were taken by means of the English Parliament, called in 1529, which were designed either to browbeat the Pope into accepting the status quo or to cut off ties with Rome altogether. Papal power in England was at first reduced and then annulled. Appeals to the Roman court and the payments owed to Rome, such as annates and Peter's Pence, were banned. The cornerstone of all these changes was the declaration that Henry was head of the Church of England, 'so far as the law of Christ would allow', an issue that led to the execution of Bishop Fisher of Rochester and the humanist Sir Thomas More for their refusal to accept the ruling.

Then, in a sense as an aftermath, Parliament passed acts dissolving all the smaller monasteries in 1536 and three years later the remainder. To reformers the monasteries may well have seemed outposts of the old regime. Thomas Cromwell, who had been given the grand title of Vicar-General, set up a commission to report on the lives and conduct of their inmates. Naturally, scandal and incompetence were highlighted.

Monasteries were certainly attracting few recruits and a small number were in acute decay but they had continued to play a valuable part in the country's religious life. Through the confiscation of their extensive properties the Crown acquired a great wealth that, apart from funding six new bishoprics, it was to fritter away as a mass of monastic land passed into the hands of lay proprietors, noble and rich merchants. They had henceforth a vested interest in the Reformation that even the Catholic Mary Tudor could not overturn.

In some parts of the country, in northern England in particular, the dissolution of the monasteries, as well as fiscal grievances, led to an armed rising known as the Pilgrimage of Grace, which at one time threatened a dangerous situation for the government. It pointed to an underlying ferment of discontent with some of the religious innovations. Governed by his own egocentric fears, Henry rid himself of Anne Boleyn. She had given Henry a daughter, the future Queen Elizabeth, but she miscarried a son, ironically on the very day of the funeral of her predecessor, Catherine of Aragon. Henry's passion was fading. Arrested on a probably trumped-up charge of adultery, she was executed. Her successor, the submissive Jane Seymour, died after giving birth to a son, the future Edward VI. For the remainder of Henry's reign the royal court became the centre of intrigue as powerful noble factions, either more Protestant or more Catholic in opinion, battled with each other for power and influence. Masterful as Henry was, convinced that his power was divinely ordained, he only doubtfully had the mastery over the religious policy that he followed.

The acrid smell of power and convulsions of policy hid the steady change in religious opinion as the country drifted more and more towards a Protestant solution of the religious problem. In an effort to shore up the Protestant cause, Thomas Cromwell sought the support of the German Protestant princes, which would help to counter improved relations between the French and the Emperor, arranging a marriage, his fourth, between Henry and Anne of Cleves, the sister of a German Protestant prince. On her arrival in England Henry discovered that she was very different from the beauty that Holbein had depicted; he had her pensioned off to an English manor and Cromwell sent to the Tower to have his head struck off. This gave an opportunity to the pro-Catholic party, led by the Duke of Norfolk, to acquire power, bolstered up, as it must have seemed, by Henry's fifth marriage to

Catherine Howard, Norfolk's niece. But Catherine was flighty and indiscreet, even taking a lover after her marriage, and when Cranmer informed the king of her indiscretion she too made her way to the block.

Through this maelstrom of continuous political uncertainty Archbishop Cranmer just managed to survive. Believing as firmly as Henry himself in the semi-divine nature of the regality, he was to be the principal architect of the English Reformation. He was not merely the master of a superb prose style, but a highly intelligent, thoughtful and sincere man. Although he had always to take his master's quirks into consideration, his own spiritual odyssey was moving in a gradual radical direction and with it went the order of the English Church. He strongly supported the reading of the Bible in English. The first translation since that of Wyclif and his associates was the masterly work of William Tyndale (who was to be put to death for heresy by the Imperialists abroad); English Bibles were soon being printed in large number as the order went out that a copy was to be placed in every English parish church.

Roman ornaments were taken down and stored away, saints' days were discontinued and other ceremonies abandoned. As a result of the current disorder the number of men seeking ordination had greatly declined but the new men who replaced the traditionalists were likely to be Protestant in their sympathies. The bench of bishops witnessed also the appointment of newcomers likely to be sympathetic to the new order of things. Slowly the Church of England was lurching towards a more emphatically Protestant settlement.

The process was slow and uncertain and must have been from the lay point of view in many ways very baffling. The Protestant party had introduced in 1536 the Ten Articles, which limited the sacraments to three – baptism, penance and the Eucharist – and stated the doctrine of justification by faith, attained by contrition and faith joined with charity. Three years later the position was reversed. The Six Articles of 1539 upheld a belief in transubstantiation, and communion in one kind, approved monastic vows and enforced clerical celibacy. Two Protestant bishops resigned and Cranmer, who had married the niece of a German reformer in 1532 thereby breaking his vow of celibacy – it was his second marriage for he had been married before he was ordained but his wife had died – had hastily to despatch Mrs Cranmer back to Germany. Norfolk and the Catholic party, however, soon fell from grace and Henry, in ailing health and relying on the good offices of his Protestant wife, Catherine Parr – whom he had married on the day of his previous wife's execution – died in 1546, holding his archbishop's hand. He was succeeded by his ten-year-old son, Edward VI.

What after some twenty years of religious reformation was the situation at the level of the parish pump? If the king seemed often confused as to what he really believed, even receiving a Catholic envoy, Bertano, at court in the last year of his life, then many of his subjects must have been in a similar position. There must have been places with long-serving parish priests where traditions of the past were maintained and life went on very much as it had done before. The North and the Cornish South-West were conservative areas, still much attached to the old faith, while East Anglia, London and the South-East, where Lollardy had had its following, became more distinctively Protestant. London, with St Paul's Cathedral – and St Paul's Cross was an influential preaching centre – and over 100 parish churches and 39 religious houses, was one of the regions most affected by religious change. Not surprisingly, it was estimated that there were more heretics in London than anywhere else in the kingdom. In 1529 the Imperial ambassador, Chapuys, commented that 'here nearly all the people hate the priests'. 'The Gospel was never more successfully preached in the time of the apostles than it hath been of late in London', Henry Brinkelow reported in 1545. Yet as elsewhere the picture remained very confused. After the enactment of the Six Articles, the French ambassador, Marillac, asserted that 'the people show great joy at the King's declaration touching the Sacrament, being much more inclined to the old religion than to the new opinions'.

However, the new opinions were seeping in, circulated by Protestant propaganda and by a growing realization of the spiritual benefits to be drawn from the reformed faith. The reading of the Bible in English for some men and women opened up a voyage of discovery. The new faith was capable of providing an intense religious experience and emotional engagement, which had a particular appeal to the younger generation, the 'lewd lads' stimulated by a movement of novelty and protest.

It was, however, by no means easy to keep one's religious balance. If one lost it, then a violent death after torture was likely to be one's fate, as Anabaptists and proto-Catholics both discovered.

'Charity', as the king had himself observed in 1545, 'between man and man is so refrigerate.' Toleration was not a concept acceptable to either side.

And now with Henry gone, having directed in his will that Masses should be said for his soul, doubtless an admirable precaution but also an expression of the strong hold that past belief still had over him, a boy no more than ten, precocious, priggish and pious, sat on the throne under the tutelage of his uncle, Somerset, a convinced evangelical. A new and significant phase in the story of the English Reformation was about to begin. 'As far as true religion is concerned', the radical Protestant Hooper told Heinrich Bullinger in Zürich in January 1546, 'idolatry is nowhere in greater vigour. Our King has destroyed the Pope not Popery.' Popery was now to be the target of the Edwardian reformers. The chantries were to go the way of the monasteries. Chantries were endowed chapels where masses were said for the souls of the dead that they might be released from the pains of Purgatory. Their dissolution meant a further increment for the Crown but for traditionalists this represented a more sinister challenge, striking at the traditional faith of the populace.

Cranmer was in his heyday. Without the sinister king looking over his shoulder the whole time, he could let his ideas flow more freely towards a more radical evangelical position. He, as well as Protector Somerset, corresponded with Zwingli's successor, Bullinger, in Zürich and with Calvin at Geneva. Some of the continental reformers were invited to come to England to canvass their faith, taking teaching posts, as Peter Martyr did at Oxford and other like-minded scholars at Cambridge, among them Martin Bucer, which would help to ensure a supply of Protestant clergy. Preachers were sent around the country to propagate the true message of the Gospel. Evangelical bishops like Hooper of Gloucester who, it was said, brought with him a whiff of Geneva and Ridley of London encouraged a preaching clergy, no easy task, for the vast majority of the English people remained wavering, uncertain and ignorant.

In any case the march towards Protestantism was to be interrupted by political crises. Somerset, a mild man and no persecutor, was confronted with an armed rising in East Anglia, in the main for economic and social reasons, and in the West Country, where people were angry with religious change. He fell victim to the ambitions of his political rival, Northumberland. The latter, a cynical politician with occasional flashes of altruism, was to assert a strong Protestantism, in some sense a cover for a further attack on the Church and its property. Cranmer, who in 1549 had prepared a new service book, the first Book of Common Prayer – in English but middle of the road in its statements – was persuaded to make a further revision, much more distinctively Protestant in its teaching, replacing a semi-sacramental view of the Eucharist by a memorialist interpretation. All these moves had the support of the young King Edward VI, the 'godly imp', pronounced by his flatterers to be a new Josiah, the benevolent ruler of ancient Israel, with which the more evangelical group liked to compare the Protestantized England. But Edward's health was poor and on 6 July 1553 he died in the arms of his attendant, Sir Henry Sidney, reciting a prayer of his own making. His successor, according to his father's will, should have been his Catholic sister, Mary, a scenario that Northumberland, ambitious for himself, could not accept, installing as queen Lady Jane Grey, the newly married wife of his son, Lord Guildford Dudley, and cousin to the late king. Northumberland's attempt to stage a coup d'état failed, for, apart from his own unpopularity, the majority of the ancient aristocracy, as well as the populace of London, opposed the usurpation and championed the right of Mary Tudor.

In a sense the English Reformation seemed to come full circle. As in a game of religious monopoly, religion had been posted back to square one. As the daughter of Catherine of Aragon, Mary was a devout Catholic, determined to reverse the religious changes of the past twenty-five years: to do away with the Protestant-inspired legislation, to encourage people to bring back images, altar cloths and the like, which they were not unwilling to do. 'Here is no news but candlesticks, books, bells, censers, crosses and pipes', commented William Dalby, 'the Mass is very rife.' The married clergy were obliged to put away their wives. The leading Protestant bishops, Latimer, Hooper and Ridley, were deprived of office, imprisoned and ultimately burned at the stake at Oxford. Archbishop Cranmer, holding as strongly as he did to the semi-divine nature of kingship, at first prevaricated but at the end stoutly affirmed his faith and courageously suffered the pains of burning. The conservative Henrician Stephen Gardiner (wily Winchester) was restored to his bishopric, Edmund Bonner to London and Mary's cousin, the scholarly Reginald Pole, was brought back from Rome to succeed Cranmer at Canterbury and, as papal legate, to restore the English Church to the Roman allegiance. A counter-revolution was in full spate. By and large a confused populace acquiesced and even greeted the restoration of the Roman connection. But Protestantism, which had garnered its own deeply committed adherents, if still a minority of the population, had no wish to kneel in the house of Baal. 'You are in the confines of Babylon', the Protestant John Philpot told his sister, 'where you are in danger to drink of the whore's cup, unless you are vigilant in prayer.' 'This Latin service', said another, John Bradford, 'is a plain mark of Antichrist's Catholic synagogue.'

Some of the clerical leaders and academics did not wait for the order to leave but made their way overseas to the Protestant sanctuaries of Strasbourg and Emden, Zürich and Geneva. Nor had Mary improved her popularity by her own marriage to the Catholic Prince Philip II of Spain. But the critics of her religious regime had to be brought to book by the fires of Smithfield. Bishop Bonner justified the executions on the ground that they were preserving the body politic from a mortal disease 'as a good surgeon [who] cutteth away a putrefed and festred member, for the love he hath to the hole body least it injecte other members adjoynynge to it.' The numbers involved were comparatively few and those who suffered were by and large ordinary people, clergy, housewives. But, like the early Christian martyrs, their deaths made an indelible impression. 'They will die with such a courage and such a trust in God it is a certain sign that they shall be saved.' They were to be commemorated for ever in John Foxe's *Book of Martyrs*, first published in 1563, which became a classic handbook for early English Protestants.

Yet their cremated remains did not challenge the regime – rather the reverse. There seemed little chance of a successful insurrection as the failure of the armed rising led by the poet and courtier Sir Thomas Wyatt in Kent showed. The restoration of Catholicism could only be challenged if the English landed classes opposed the regime, but they still looked to the royal court as the fount of honour and profit. Mary and Pole had neither sufficient time to promote the reforms in the Church that they had in mind nor the requisite financial backing and political aptitude; Pole died on the evening of

17 November 1558, a few hours after the queen, who had been ill for some time. Had Mary lived to her sister Elizabeth's age (Elizabeth was seventy when she died, Mary was only forty-two) the Roman Catholic faith might well have been successfully reinstated in England and the English Reformation would have been the Reformation that failed, for its roots were still shallow.

Mary's sister Elizabeth, the daughter of Henry VIII and Anne Boleyn, was something of an unknown quantity. Obviously sympathetic to the religious changes made by her father, she had to tread delicately. In religious matters too she was conservative, remaining a Henrician rather than an Edwardian. It was inconceivable that she would be reconciled to Rome for, apart from anything else, she was by canon law illegitimate. Yet she had a liking for traditional ceremonial and if she was suspicious of Catholics as her potential enemies she was no friend to Protestant extremists. She was to follow in religious matters a policy of via media.

The Marian exiles returned eager for power and position but while some gained recognition they were rather coolly received. Moreover the middle way which the queen sought to follow was probably the policy that, with some exceptions, the nobility and the landed gentry were ready to support and which her people by persuasion, supervision and coercion came to accept. She had found a judicious head of the English Church in a former Cambridge don, Matthew Parker, who set about restoring some of the Edwardian usages that Mary had abolished. An Act of Supremacy declared that Elizabeth was Supreme Governor (but tactfully, in view of her sex, not the Head as Henry had been) of the Church of England; an Act of Uniformity made a happy conflation of the two prayer books of Cranmer, so that it was even possible to opt for either a sacramental or a memorialist interpretation of the Eucharist. The pro-Roman bishops were replaced by a series of conscientious, time-serving prelates, some of whom, like Jewell of Salisbury, were scholarly evangelicals. They were one and all the queen's men, unable to prevent the royal treasury from time to time filching parts of their episcopal estates. They sought to ensure that the parish priests in their dioceses conformed and that their parishioners attended the church services as they were bound to do, offenders being brought before the Church courts. The universities of Oxford and

Cambridge, at last purged of Romanists, set about training the country's future Protestant pastors. So Elizabeth's long reign provided the time and the opportunity to ensure that Protestantism was integrated into the national heritage, its doctrinal position defined in the 39 Articles of 1571 and finding an intellectual justification in the *Laws of Ecclesiastical Polity* written by the 'judicious' Richard Hooker; this brought together the tenets of the modern evangelical Protestant faith in an elegant mix that admitted the validity of the Church's patristic past, finding the foundation of the Church's teaching in Scripture, the early Church fathers and the early Councils of the Church, tradition and reason. Ultimately the English Reformation was a compromise, a hybrid, a marriage settlement between Catholic antiquity and Protestant principle, a solvent that was to determine the future history of the Church of England.

At the time this seemed less than a settled solution. The majority of the population was probably more apathetic than enthusiastic and might have still opted for the 'old religion' but with the passing of the generations – the old dying off and the once young, educated in the Protestant tradition, taking their place – a more distinctively Protestant Church came into being.

If Elizabeth had sleepless nights about religious issues, they may well have been caused by the demands of the more extreme Protestants, their ideals taken from the Church in Geneva. Suspicious of episcopal order, they appealed to the authority of Scripture interpreted literally, opposing the continued usage of ceremonial practices like the wearing of vestments, kneeling to receive communion and the giving of the ring in marriage. This group, who became in time more generally known as the Puritans, were loquacious and demanding, expressing their views in a pamphlet literature, widely read and often virulent in tone. The queen had herself made a serious blunder in selecting Archbishop Parker's successor, for Edmund Grindal was himself mildly Puritan in his sympathies and lost favour. With relief she turned to a more determined successor, the vigorous John Whitgift, the former Master of Trinity College, Cambridge, whose views on religious dissent were similar to her own. He introduced a Court of High Commission, which dealt harshly with ecclesiastical offenders and came down heavily on subversive pamphlets like the Marprelate Tracts that queried the Church settlement and demanded further reform in a radical direction. Puritanism was a portmanteau word that covered a very wide-ranging set of views, from calls for moderate reform to more extreme measures. It was more or less contained in Elizabeth's reign but not eliminated, proving a very powerful force in the first half of the next century. A few extreme Puritan groups like the Brownists, to avoid persecution, emigrated to the safer territory of the Low Countries.

If Puritanism was to be increasingly influential, Roman Catholicism, still strong in some parts of the country, especially in northern England and Sussex, where it had support from some of the landed gentry, was politically in decline. Its adherents had been rallied by the devoted services of the so-called missionary priests trained at continental seminaries like Douai and sent to provide religious services for the faithful, but their arrival seemed to many Englishmen only to underline Catholicism's foreign character. Catholicism suffered from its identification with the common enemy, Spain, whose king, Philip II, Mary Tudor's husband, was the champion of the Catholic cause, from Catholic involvement in plots against Elizabeth, by the papal condemnation of Elizabeth in 1570, and by the support that Catholics gave to Mary Queen of Scots. Under Archbishop Whitgift's lead the full rigour of the law was applied to bring Catholics into line. Catholicism could not be outlawed but Catholics, under penalty of a fine, were obliged to attend Protestant religious services and for those, like the missionary priests, believed guilty of treason, execution was the final penalty, adding a further number, if fewer than the sufferers under the Marian regime, of martyrs for their faith.

Although the Roman Catholics were to remain a substantial minority, they became for the most part loyal to the Crown as their support for Charles I in the Civil War was to show. Puritanism remained a significant force in English religious life, bursting into fuller flood under the early Stuart kings. Yet Elizabeth's reign had seen the Church of England take permanent shape. In so far as such matters are historically measurable, England had become a Protestant country. To all intents and purposes after some seventy years of alternating fortune the English Reformation was complete and there was no possibility of a reversal.

FIVE

John Calvin & the Reformation in Geneva

John Calvin was a northern Frenchman from Picardy. Geneva, a semi-independent city that had fallen under Savoyard influence, did not actually become a Swiss canton until 1814. But no one better epitomized the Swiss Reformation than Calvin. He was born on 10 July 1509 at Noyon where his father, Gérard, was a lawyer in the employment of the local bishop, and obtained for his son two small benefices, the income from which helped to pay for his education. In 1523 John went to study in Paris, attending the Collège de Montaigu where Erasmus had once been a student and where the founder of the Jesuits, Ignatius Loyola, was to reside. Calvin may have been originally intended for the priesthood, but as his father had clashed acrimoniously with the cathedral authorities at Noyon, it was decided that he should study law.

He studied law at Orléans under the eminent Pierre L'Estoile, taking his doctorate there in 1532 and then, beckoned by the high reputation of the legal scholar Alciat, he transferred to Bourges. His life, as his friend and future biographer Theodore Beza remembered, was laborious and austere, so much so that he undermined his health. At Bourges he became friends with a fellow student, Melchior Wolmar, a German who had studied at Berne and become a Lutheran sympathizer who, it was said, first 'poisoned the mind of the young man with heresy'. Calvin's study of the law may account for the later legalistic traits in his theology and certainly helped to make him a precise logician but his early interests were humanistic and classical rather than theological, his first published work in 1532 being a commentary on Seneca's *De Clementia*.

Calvin was certainly aware of the contemporary ferment in the Church and was himself moving slowly in the direction of reform. In late 1533 he had been involved, exactly how is not clear, in an indiscreet sermon that his friend Nicholas Cop, Rector of the University of Paris, had preached on All Saints' Day, contrasting the slavery of the law with the saving merits of Christ's sacrifice, and thus appearing to minimize

71

the importance of good works in the scheme of salvation. Cop thought it wiser to leave for Basle, a city already acting as host to religious reformers.

The reaction in France against the spread of reformed ideas was gathering pace. Some supporters of reform had audaciously plastered Paris (and even the royal castle at Amboise) with 'placards' imported from Switzerland, attacking 'les horribles, grands et impudentes abus de la mese papale'. Some of the miscreants were caught and burned at the stake.

In this climate of opinion Calvin thought that he had better move to a more sympathetic terrain. He may already have undergone a conversion experience, for in his later commentary on the Psalms, he averred that he had been 'tamed by God', who had brought his heart to docility, leading him to the true doctrine that he felt obliged to impart to others. With his friend du Tillet, travelling under assumed names, they took refuge first in Strasbourg, then in Basle where he met other foreign reformers, among them Bullinger from Zürich, before moving on to northern Italy to visit the Duchess of Ferrara, Renée, a first cousin of the French king, known to be sympathetic to the reformed cause, presumably in the hope that she might take up the cause of his co-religionists in

France. From Italy Calvin returned to Basle, taking advantage of a semi-amnesty to pay a last visit to France to fulfil some family legal business. He then intended to return to Strasbourg but as his passage was blocked by Imperial troops he made a detour that brought him to the lakeside city of Geneva.

Geneva's recent history had been confused and violent. The city had originally enjoyed a measure of self-government but was subject to the bishop and fell under the power of the neighbouring Duchy of Savoy. It had recently managed to throw off the Savoyard yoke with the support of the canton of Berne, now a stronghold of the reformed faith. Consequently, the Council of Geneva began to favour the new ideas. An ardent reformer, Guillaume Farel, was invited to become preacher at the Church of St Gervais. The council was persuaded to ban the Mass, to dissolve the monasteries and to impose tough moral edicts outlawing blasphemy, card-playing and dice and obliging the citizens under penalty of a fine to attend sermons. When Calvin arrived in Geneva he was invited by Farel, already a friend, to stay and help consolidate the religious revolution there.

Appointed by the council as Reader in Holy Scripture at the Church of St Pierre, in spite of severe attacks of catarrh and neuralgia, Calvin soon had opportunities to demonstrate the power of his mind and the determination of his will. In Geneva he began to show his mastery, drawing up a new catechism, ensuring that evil-doers were excluded from communion and obliging citizens to subscribe to a Confession of Faith. Geneva's allies, the Bernese, were alarmed by the uncompromising stand that Calvin and Farel were taking and had the support of the reformers' opponents in Geneva. The council ordered Calvin and Farel to accept the rites of the Church of Berne. When, in 1538, the two reformers excommunicated their critics they were ordered to leave the city.

Farel eventually made his way to Neuchâtel while Calvin returned, on Bucer's invitation, to minister in Strasbourg where the churches were swinging from a Lutheran to a Zwinglian position. There Calvin married Idalette de Bure, the widow of a former Anabaptist and by whom he had two children, but his circumstances were such that he had to supplement his meagre stipend by taking in pensionnaires. In Geneva there was reaction in favour of Farel, whose supporters won power and executed the leaders of the Bernese faction. Calvin had settled happily in

Strasbourg and was reluctant to accept an invitation to come back to Geneva but he returned to the city on 13 September 1541, taking an oath 'to be for ever the servant of Geneva'.

He had begun to write his epochal work *The Institutes of the Christian Religion*, which was to become the textbook of the majority of the reformed churches, when he was at Basle. Published in 1536 with a dedication to Francis I of France, in six chapters, it was to be constantly revised and extended, amounting to some twenty-four chapters by 1550. The basis of Calvin's faith was his belief in the absolute sovereignty of God and, as a corollary, the worthlessness of man. God's will, inscrutable yet omniscient, was visualized as the centre of the moral order and the lynch-pin of creation. By his very nature, God must be remote from sinful humanity, human sin originating with Adam's fall in the Garden of Eden when he took fruit from the forbidden tree. Sin was so all-pervasive that it was impossible for man to save himself. Only divine intervention could provide an opportunity for this for those who were predestined or elected to salvation. For man, sinful as he undoubtedly was, nevertheless possessed the moral self-knowledge that enabled him to recognize his shortcomings. The work of the Spirit will imbue man with the fear that will lead him to a wish to repent. However, this depends ultimately on God's initiative. At the basis of this was the belief in the doctrine of predestination, a belief that most of the reformers accepted. The doctrine of election or predestination, 'decretum quidem horribilis', did not, as one might suppose, engender a feeling of religious fatalism but inspired a high degree of religious enthusiasm on the part of believers and a determination to show by their good works proof of their election.

For the next twenty-three years Calvin sought to put such ideas to practical application in the city of Geneva. With his scraggy beard (beards seem to have been a necessary adjunct for most reforming ministers), thin lips, unhealthy pallor and intense eyes, Calvin was not only a charismatic figure but a man with an iron will and irresistible power. He reorganized the Church and disciplined the people. His very first act was to appoint a committee of ministers and councillors who drew up the *Ordonnances Ecclésiastiques*, which were approved by the Great Council in 1541. These were intended to be in conformity with the supposed *ordo* of the Primitive Church as revealed in the Pauline Epistles.

Their execution was purely a matter for the Church, and the powers of the state were only to be invoked in special emergency.

The Church was to be governed by four orders of pastors, known as the Venerable Company, doctors, deacons and elders. The city was itself divided into three parishes, St Pierre, St Gervais and the Madeleine. Due provision was made for Sunday and weekday services and for the catechetical instruction of the young, for whose education the doctors were to be responsible, assisted in this work by the deacons who were also supposed to visit the sick and to help with the relief of the poor. The elders, twelve in number, like the Apostles, were to be elected from the three city councils (the Little Council, the Sixty and the Two Hundred or Great Council). The system was all-embracing though the Great Council, proud as it was of its minister, did not wish to surrender totally its authority over such matters.

At the heart of the disciplinary system was the Consistory; meeting every Thursday, it consisted of the ministers and twelve elders, and dealt with all breaches of discipline. Minor offences could be punished by spiritual weapons such as admonition, reprimand and exclusion from the Lord's Supper (though the wrangle over excommunication continued and was not fully resolved in Calvin's favour until 1553). For more serious offences the guilty party was handed over to the council.

The Consistory was a powerful body evoking fear and hostility, especially as it was no respecter of persons. It was accused of encouraging espionage and delation. Yet, austere as was the moral discipline enforced by Calvin in Geneva, many other churches, Catholic as well as Protestant, had long imposed penalties for moral offences. Enforcement in Geneva, however, seems to have been more efficient and the penalties more severe. It was estimated in the 1560s that no fewer than five offenders were excommunicated every week.

At a meeting early in Calvin's time at Geneva, on 16 February 1542, a woman was admonished who had knelt on her husband's grave and cried out 'Requiescat in pace'. Another, who had tried to cure her husband by tying round his neck a walnut in which she had placed a spider, was rebuked for sorcery. Later cases refer to a man who was sent to prison after insisting that he was perfectly entitled to beat his wife. Another, who had gone hunting and cursed his son and God because he had allowed a fox to escape, was imprisoned for three days to subsist on bread and water.

Three young workmen, who had over-indulged by eating three dozen pâtés endured a similar fate. Of six boys charged with unnatural vice, the youngest was sent to be beaten and the older boys burned in effigy and sentenced to three months' solitary confinement chained to a wall, a better fate than that of a man charged with the same offence who was burned to death.

The penalty for fornication had been fixed originally at three days in the local prison, the Evêché, but was increased to six days and the payment of a fine. Edicts abolished taverns, replacing them with eating houses or abbayes where grace had to be said before meals, play-acting was virtually banned, and the use of the name Claude was forbidden because it might remind people of an image of St Claude once held in veneration. Jacques Gruet, who had earlier been found guilty of dancing and of describing Calvin as having the airs of a bishop and who had apparently justified fornication (and seems indeed to have been a free thinker), was sentenced to the torture of the strapade and beheaded. Raoul Monet, a Secretary of Justice, who was convicted of carrying about a book of obscene pictures that he called his New Testament, was executed. In the autumn of 1551 Jerome Bolsec, a former Carmelite friar practising as a physician, criticized Calvin's doctrine of redemption. Bolsec had committed the worst of offences challenging right belief, and Calvin, who had spoken vainly for an hour in the hope of converting him to the right way, described him as a 'monster vomiting forth poison'. Banished from Geneva Bolsec returned to Catholicism and exacted a sort of revenge by asserting that Calvin had left France to escape a charge of sodomy.

Then came the scandal of the Servetus case. Servetus was a scholarly Spaniard and a practising physician who had the audacity to query the orthodox doctrine of the Trinity in a book, *De Trinitatis erroribus*, published in 1551, so raising the ire equally of the Spanish Inquisition and the Protestant reformers. For his subversive religious views the Inquisitor ordered Servetus's arrest, but he managed to escape and the Inquisitor had to be content with burning him in effigy. On an impulse, en route, as he stated, to Italy, he foolishly came to Geneva, where he was arrested. The charges against him, described in some forty articles, were supported by Bullinger from Zürich and the council at Geneva condemned him to be burned to death.

In spite of the firm control that Calvin and his associates exerted over the life of the city, opposition formed around a group known as the Libertins, led by Philippe Berthelier; but following a riot they were suspected of instigating, Berthelier fled abroad and others were executed.

With the defeat of his critics, Calvin's authority was left unchallenged. Yet he held no official position in the government, only in 1559 being admitted to the rights of the bourgeoisie and so becoming a full citizen of Geneva. Under his direction, the city had become the most highly organized stronghold of Protestantism in Europe. His position in the city had been greatly strengthened by the immigration of French refugees – 289 in 1551; 335 in 1553; and 517 between 1549 and 1559 – in the main hard-working, responsible people who helped to develop the economic life of Geneva. The Collège de Genève, inaugurated on 5 June 1559 though not actually completed until 1564, provided instruction in the faith for future pastors who would take their message into other lands. By 1564 it had 1,500 members, most of whom were foreigners.

Calvin's position was latterly unchallenged but his life was lonely and austere. When he returned to

Geneva he had been given a house, furnished and rent free, together with free cloth and fur for a robe, with a salary of 510 florins, later raised to 600 florins, a comparatively modest reward. With the passage of time his lifestyle did not change. His wife had died in March 1549 after suffering much ill health. Calvin's own health was poor; he was afflicted by constant migraines and probably by pulmonary tuberculosis. Yet he was a man of seemingly indestructible industry, dictating a vast correspondence with reformers abroad and in Switzerland, in particular with Bullinger in Zürich, and continuing to write his Biblical Commentaries. His death on 27 May 1564 marked the end of an era but there was to be no lull in the worldwide influence that his teaching continued to exert. His dedication to the Gospel of Jesus Christ, however he interpreted it, was unquestionable. He had, in the view of the Scottish reformer John Knox, created 'the most perfect school of Christ that ever was on earth since the days of the Apostles'. If his critics were treated harshly, to the majority of the citizens his dedicated life was seemingly a lesson in Christian discipleship.

SIX

The Spread of Calvinism

The expansion of Lutheranism was halted and even delimited by the advance of Calvinism, which was to become the supreme international force in the plantation of the European Reformation, its mainspring in France, the Low Countries, in Scotland and later in North America. Calvinism's potency was largely derived from its systematic theology and its superior organization. Calvin, like Luther, stressed man's basic depravity and his consequent inability to achieve salvation without the saving power of Christ. Both were believers in predestination but in Calvinism the belief in election seemed to give the Calvinist a prophetic and crusading edge. Convinced of the righteousness of their cause, the Calvinists believed that they were carrying out God's work against the world, the flesh and the Devil.

Together with this strong, overriding faith there went a potent organization of which the Church in

Geneva was the prototype. Calvinist churches were governed by a series of elected bodies: the local consistory or synod, the presbytery, the colloquy or classis and higher up the scale the provincial and national synods, constituting a series of concentric circles which ensured that Calvinism would be a strong political as well as a spiritual force.

Calvinism became the basis of the reform movement in France. The Reformation's course in France was to be violent, cruel and often confused, but in spite of strong counter-attacks by its opponents, it was to make substantial headway.

At first sight there seemed to be no particular reason why France should not have experienced a successful religious revolution. The early reformers in France had had a smattering of royal patronage in the person of the king's sister, Marguerite d'Angoulême, who briefly befriended the reforming prelate Guillaume Briçonnet, Bishop of Meaux, and his vicar-general, the humanist Jacques Lèfevre d'Etaples, who seemed to have accepted a view of justification similar to that held by Luther and who penned a translation of the New Testament into French. But this small coterie never had an effective following and was soon put to flight. Briçonnet recanted and Lèfevre hied off to Geneva.

It certainly seemed possible that the small groups attracted to reform could not have kept the flame of reform alive if it had not been for John Calvin. Calvin, who had originally dedicated the first edition of his *Institutes* to King Francis I, never lost interest in his own country. Geneva was to become the centre of the Protestant mission to France, whence came colporteurs bearing a stream of Protestant literature and later pastors trained in the Calvinist tradition.

The reform movement in France grew through a process of infiltration but it won its adherents by the infection of evangelical enthusiasm. Between 1555 and 1562, 80 pastors working in France came from Geneva and in 1561/2 there were reckoned to be some 150 reformed congregations. These were already grouped into religious organizations based on the Geneva model. A national synod was first held at Paris in 1559 and within a few years, as well as a national synod, there were provincial synods and colloquies knitting together the scattered congregations.

The growth in numbers was sufficient to pressurize the Church and state to take action to repress heresy. Under Francis I's successor, Henry II, new laws were instituted for the apprehension and trial of heretics; the edict of Châteaubriant in 1551 laid down that those accused of heresy should be deprived of judicial or municipal office.

It was plain that these measures had proved inadequate to stem Protestantism's growth. If it had failed to win royal support it had some strong backers among a few of the higher nobility, notably Antoine de Bourbon (whose wife, Jeanne d'Albret, was the daughter of Marguerite d'Angoulême), Louis, Prince de Condé, Gaspar II de Coligny, Admiral of France, and his brother, Odet de Châtillon, Cardinal Bishop of Beauvais. By their power and patronage, these men gave their support to public demonstrations of reform such as the psalm singing that went on for three days in Paris in 1558. Such highly born supporters may have been sincerely convinced of the truth of their new-found faith but some at least of the lesser landowners were drawn to the support of the reformed cause in the hope that an attack on the property of the Church might help to rehabilitate their fortunes affected by the current depression.

On the whole, reformed opinion was stronger in urban areas than in the countryside. Middle-class men and women were attracted not merely by the spiritual message of Calvinism but also by its ethical teaching with its emphasis on thrift, industry and family values.

Of 561 people at a Huguenot service in November 1560, 36 were city notables, 24 were merchants, 87 were lawyers, physicians and apothecaries, 387 were artisans and shopkeepers including some 135 textile workers, and 27 were peasant farmers. The spread of the reformed faith was cellular in character, spreading from group to group.

However, by the middle of the sixteenth century it might have appeared that a religious stalemate had been reached. The Catholic Church in France, not yet rejuvenated by the Counter-Reformation, could only respond to its critics with imprisonment and death. The Crown, now embodied in the person of the queen mother, Catherine de Medici, acting as regent for her young son, Charles IX, and a woman of no strong religious principles, came to favour a compromise that would satisfy the competing parties and so avert the growing threat of civil war. She called a meeting of theologians of both sides in Poissy near Paris in September 1561 but it broke up without a settlement. Next year, in a further effort to avert a conflict, she issued an edict at Saint Germain-des-Près that granted limited rights of assembly and worship to the Huguenots, as the adherents of the reformed faith had come to be called, a nickname said to have been imported from Geneva and derived from the German *eidgenoss* or confederate. The Catholic partisans became increasingly alarmed by the growth in the number of Huguenot congregations and the seeming policy of appeasement followed by the Crown. In March 1562 an armed attack by the Duke of Guise, an ardent Catholic supporter, on a Protestant congregation at Vassy left seventy-four dead.

France was descending into the darkness of a long and savage period of thirty years of intermittent religious warfare. The wars were regional in their incidence but bloody in character, interrupted by negotiated peaces that stood no real chance of being implemented permanently and were really no more than truces. In 1572 Catherine de Medici, jealous of the influence that the Huguenot noble Coligny was exercising over the mind of her impressionable and weak son Charles IX, instigated his assassination on St Bartholomew's Eve. The event sparked a general massacre of the Huguenots in Paris and in other towns. The Pope and the Spanish king sent their warm congratulations but Protestant princes naturally reacted in horror. It settled nothing. When, two years later, Charles IX died, his brother, Henry III, a homosexual dilettante, was not much concerned with religious issues. When he was stabbed to death in 1589 by a Dominican friar in the same year that his mother died, his successor, Henry IV, King of Navarre, of the Bourbon line of princes, was a Huguenot.

The religious wars in France had by now assumed some of the features of an international conflict, with the Spanish king, Philip II, acting as the champion of the Catholic powers in alliance with the French Catholic League while Protestant sympathizers in England, the Low Countries and Germany supported the Huguenots. In some sense, Henry IV inherited the 'politique' policy of Catherine de Medici, seeking a settlement that would terminate the distressing and ruinous conflict and allow his fellow Huguenots to practise their faith. In 1593, politically realistic, he became a convert to the Catholic faith, a diplomatic move that paved the way for settlement in the Edict of Nantes, which guaranteed liberty of conscience throughout France and gave the Huguenots the right of access to all hospitals, universities and schools; Catholics were allowed to worship freely in Catholic towns and Huguenots in all towns where they had been able to do so between January 1596 and August 1597, though they were still debarred from doing so in Paris and its immediate vicinity. The Edict of

Nantes provided a practical solution and at least brought peace to a divided country, enabling Henry and his intelligent minister, Sully, to take steps to revitalize the economy. It was an uneasy compromise, which was brought to an end when in 1685 Louis XIV, in an act of uncharacteristic devotion and political stupidity, revoked it, sending many members of this hard-working section of the urban community into exile to England and the Low Countries. Yet whatever its shortcomings, the Edict of Nantes had been an important step on the road to religious toleration.

If the Reformation had fallen short of what its adherents would have wished in France, the story of the Reformation in the Low Countries followed a rather different route. The seventeen provinces that made up the Low Countries at the start of the sixteenth century were divided by politics, language and custom; in the northern half Dutch influence was most apparent, while in the south the language and culture was Flemish and French. The cities, made rich through the textile industry, had managed to preserve their privileges and independence against a series of overlords. The Netherlands had become a part of the inheritance of the Emperor Charles V, who strongly supported the repression of heresy. Even so, through close proximity to Germany, Lutheran ideas and the radical Anabaptists infiltrated the Netherlands. Early Protestantism seemed, however, to lack a measure of coherence and even cohesion. When Charles V abdicated, his successor, the strongly Catholic Philip II, was determined to root out heresy.

The situation was made the more complex by factors that were only peripherally religious. Philip II, aware of the inefficiency of the existing diocesan system in the Netherlands, decided to remodel it, at once stirring up a hornet's nest in some part because the nobility saw the move as an attack on their own vested interests and privileges, but even more so because people feared that it augured the introduction of the much-feared Spanish Inquisition, the vehicle that Philip had utilized in Spain to suppress heresy and to sustain the power of the Crown. As a consequence, there was rising opposition to Spanish influence. More or less simultaneously, Calvinism began to win adherents under the lead of Guy de Brès, a Hainaulter who had worked in both London and Switzerland. Calvinism spread especially in the French-speaking areas of the Netherlands, giving coherence to a movement of religious dissent that had hitherto been somewhat inchoate.

The Governor of the Netherlands, King Philip's aunt, Margaret of Parma, advised by the judicious Cardinal Granvelle, had, like Catherine de Medici, no wish to alienate the powerful nobility but they could hardly avoid implementing Philip's religious policy. One of the leaders among the nobility, Count Egmont, petitioned Philip to modify the heresy laws but Philip was a devout doctrinaire, who responded by ordering the edicts against heresy to be sternly enforced. At this stage a number of nobles supported a move made by Philippe Marnix de Ste Aldegonde, a serious Calvinist who had drawn up a document known as the Compromise, which called for religious toleration. In some of the cities afflicted by unemployment, workers were inflamed by the reformed preachers and in the summer of 1566 formed mobs that sacked churches, destroying ornaments and images. The threat of violence alarmed some of the nobility, among them Egmont, who made his peace with Philip, but the future leader of the Protestant revolt, William, Prince of Orange-Nassau, thought it wiser to seek the safety of his German estates from where he could give his support to reform.

Philip had learned his lesson and replaced Duchess Margaret as governor-general by a hardline soldier, the Duke of Alva, who introduced a policy of brutal repression. The resistance to Spain, though still largely political, began to take on a more strongly religious tinge as the militants' fervour was whipped up by Calvinist preachers. Anti-Spanish feeling was strongest in the maritime province of Holland.

Compromise was no longer a political or a religious option but Alva's plans for a massive repressive policy were overtaken by the dangerous state of the Spanish economy, so depressed that it could no longer bear the cost of fighting an expensive war. The unpaid Spanish troops mutinied and in 1576 sacked Antwerp.

If Philip had lost the initiative, he had not yet lost the war. While religious fervour was as strong as ever, helping to ferment a further rebellion in Ghent in the south, divisions among the provinces where particularism was deep-rooted deprived the rebels of complete victory. In the south a compromise was reached which helped to ensure that Catholicism would remain dominant there while the new governor-general, Duchess Margaret's son, Alessandro, Duke of Parma, proved a capable general who kept the southern provinces loyal and Catholic.

It was a different story in the north, for in 1581, having renounced their allegiance to Philip, the States-General of the Netherlands looked round for a suitable head to replace him, playing disastrously with the notion of nominating a French prince. Finally, it fell back on William of Orange, who became Stadtholder of the United Provinces and was succeeded after his murder in 1584 by his brother, Maurice. Finally, in 1609, a truce was negotiated with Spain that twelve years later led to the recognition of the independence of the northern states.

This complex story was a heavy mixture of politics and religion interfused by particularist sentiment. Religious zeal had converged with the desire for political independence to enable the Dutch to win the battle against Spain after a drawn-out conflict. The initiative had been taken by an enthusiastic minority, but as time went on they were reinforced by allies, some from outside the Netherlands. In particular, there was a stream of preachers, many trained in Geneva where they had fled from presecution – some 60,000, it was estimated, during Alva's governor-generalship – while others came from France, Germany and England, where by 1572 there were seventeen communities of Calvinist refugees. A depression in trade and the high cost of bread added to the discontent on which the preachers and their allies could work. A church organized on Calvinist lines provided the means by which a dominant minority could gain the upper hand. Calvinism provided the backbone of the resistance to Spain and helped to secure the attainment of independence.

Beneath the surface, however, there were some conflicting voices. Against the rigorists who accepted Calvinist teaching on predestination in its most rigid form there were those who held a more moderate interpretation. The clash of opinion became bitter but was to result in victory for the rigorists at the Synod of Dort in 1618. The Dutch Reformed Church, moulded in so hot a furnace, was to remain strongly Calvinist both in doctrine and in its stern moral outlook, in spite of a few dissenters, becoming a major force in the religious and cultural life of the Netherlands and eventually in South Africa, whereas the southern provinces were loyal to the old faith.

Scotland was the other country where Calvinism took a deep-rooted hold. Throughout its course the Scots Reformation was a complex amalgam of religious division interfused with political rivalry. The Scots royal family, the Stuarts, inherited an alliance with the French as a safeguard against English interference, an alliance that was cemented by the marriage of the youthful Scots queen, Mary, to the French king, Francis II. The Scots royal family was likely to give its strong support to the

Catholic Church in its struggle against the reformers.

In Scotland there had long been pockets of religious unrest to which abuses in the Church contributed, with the result that it proved receptive to reformed ideas from the Continent. In 1525 the importation of Lutheran literature was banned. A Scottish abbot, Patrick Hamilton, went to Marburg to study, composed a short Lutheran tract and on his return was burned as a heretic at St Andrews in 1528. But other intellectuals were to follow him abroad. Authority remained, however, concerned to put down reform. The burnings continued, with the friar George Wishart suffering in 1546 though his fate was later to be revenged by the brutal murder of Archbishop David Beaton.

Nevertheless, the slow tide of Protestantism crept in. Local churches, 'privy kirks', were organized that followed the English liturgical practices of 1552. Some Scottish nobles with a greedy eye on church property came together to form the militant Lords of the Congregation. This more or less coincided with the return to Scotland of the pugnacious reformer John Knox. Knox had served as a captive on French galleys, studying after his release at Geneva where he absorbed strong Calvinist views. Gaining a reputation as a fervent preacher he was invited to preach before Edward VI at the English court before he came back to Scotland, where he preached at Perth and instigated the destruction of images and religious houses. A clever and charismatic firebrand, he was to be the principal force behind Scotland's move into the Protestant camp.

With English support, Elizabeth having recently become queen, the Lords of the Congregation attained power in 1560 and at their behest the Scottish parliament passed laws banning the Mass and adopting a Scottish Confession of Faith along Calvinist lines. The First Book of Discipline, partly compiled under Knox's guidance, set about reorganizing the property of the Church and provided for the appointment of superintendents on the Genevan model to oversee the clergy. An English service book was adopted in 1562.

All this was taking place against a sultry political background, for the head of state, Mary, now the widowed Queen of France, remained devoted to Catholicism but she was to become an increasingly isolated figure, her reputation soiled by sexual scandal. Her army's defeat by the Lords of the Congregation at

Carberry Hill in 1567 was followed by her flight to England and subsequent long imprisonment by Queen Elizabeth (and eventual execution in 1585), so paving the way for the slow dismantling of the Catholic establishment and the appointment of committed Protestants to high offices in Church and state.

The situation remained confused, for there was acute disagreement as to how far the newly reformed Church should be self-governing, as in Geneva, or how far along English lines it should be subordinate to the authority of the state. The pendulum was to swing now one way and then the other. The intellectual spokesman for the Presbyterian model was Andrew Melville, who became Principal of Glasgow University in 1574 and who is perhaps best known for describing his king, James VI (soon to be James I of England), as 'God's silly vassal'. The struggle was to continue during most of the seventeenth century but the Presbyterian system, much assisted by the outcome of the English Civil War, eventually triumphed. The Church of Scotland fully accepted Calvinist doctrine and its moral discipline, which continued to be its life-blood.

Yet Calvinism was never completely free of dissent. In Holland there had been a bitter struggle between the so-called Remonstrants and Contra-Remonstrants over predestination, which issued in the victory of the rigorists. In Scotland in the nineteenth century there was to be a division as, in 1843, the able Calvinist theologian Thomas Chalmers, fearful that the self-government of the Church was threatened by interference from the civil courts, led a secessionist movement, resulting in the setting up of the Free Church of Scotland. By contrast, four years earlier in the Netherlands, Abraham Kuyper headed a secession in the Dutch Reformed Church against what he felt to be its unacceptable liberalizing tendencies. Ten years later a similar secession took place in the Church of Geneva led by Merle d'Aubigné. In France the Eglise Reformée Evangelique was formed in opposition to the official Huguenot body, the Eglise Reformée de France, partly because the critics felt that it enjoyed too much support from the state.

Although such divisions show that, since Calvin's day, there has been a theological tension between the more conservative and more liberal interpreters of his teaching, they do not deflect from the massive influence that Calvinism has exerted on the religious scene worldwide.

SEVEN

The Protestant Underground

Throughout the history of Christianity there have always been small groups of believers who have drawn novel theological and social notions from their readings of Scripture that diverged from orthodox teaching. They were often obsessed with the Second Coming of Christ and the Last Judgement when the elect would be vindicated, and in the belief that this might happen in the near future they would set up a church of true believers, separate from those who, they supposed, had been 'misled' by false teachers whether Protestant or Catholic. With the example of the early Church in mind, they often practised a simple communism, were pacifistic and averse to the authority of the state. As they insisted on adult baptism, opposing infant baptism because the child could not understand the promises that were being made on his or her behalf, they were generically called Anabaptists. These sects were not a phenomenon confined to the period of the Reformation; millenarian hopes have been expressed at all periods and perhaps have never been more widespread than in the many sects of twentieth-century America and Africa.

However, these sects have tended to come into existence at times of stress and ferment and some could be viewed as the illegitimate progeny of the Reformation. While they occasionally even found some support in princely courts their appeal was by and large to the depressed sections of the community, workers and peasants beguiled by the colourful oratory, often drawn from the Book of Revelation, of their prophets, with the promise of better times that the Second Coming would herald.

Their leaders were usually clerics or ex-clerics, more learned than their followers but fanatical and messianic in their attitude. They stood little or no chance, in a worldly sense, of putting their ideas into practice and on the few occasions when they achieved power the experiment was invariably disastrous. They were the underdogs or underground of the Reformation, as much disliked and persecuted by the Protestants as by the Catholics.

As the Anabaptist missionaries often moved from one place to another, sectarianism flared up in many parts of Europe. In south-west Germany the Peasants' War of 1524–5, if ultimately social and economic in its origins, had absorbed a religious message drawn in part, much to his anger, from Luther's own teaching. The peasants acquired a powerful and charismatic leader in Thomas Müntzer, a former Lutheran pastor who in the course of a peripatetic existence was to launch a series of religious bombshells. When he had been at Allstedt in 1525 he had produced a German service book declaring that through dreams and visions the 'elect', inspired by the Holy Spirit, were called upon to establish the rule of the godly, using violence to achieve their end if necessary. Execrated by the local nobles as well as the Lutheran preachers, Müntzer moved on to foster the religious revolution in Mühlhausen and then to lead the army of militant peasants with false hopes drawn from his apocalyptic vision of the New Jerusalem. He managed to escape from the battlefield of Frankenhausen where the peasant army was defeated, only to suffer execution.

Martin Luther had strongly condemned the peasants and their leader. Zwingli too was confronted by Anabaptist trouble in Zürich. A group of his followers there, dissatisfied with what they felt to be the slow progress of reform in Zürich, denounced infant baptism, only to draw on themselves the wrath of the magistrates. The trouble-makers were first arrested and then expelled from the city. When they continued to insist on the necessity of re-baptism for admission to the Church, one of their leaders, Felix Mantz, was sentenced to be drowned in the river Limmat. His colleague, Blaurock, was expelled after flogging but later suffered execution at the hands of the Austrians.

Similar groups flourished in southern Germany and in Moravia. Influenced by the visionary teaching of Müntzer, Hans Denck preached Anabaptism in Franconia but on moving to Strasbourg he was expelled by the city magistrates. In company with Ludwig Hetzer and Melchior Rinck, two preachers of similar views, the Anabaptists won over a sufficient following to hold a conference at Augsburg in 1527, only to suffer arrest and expulsion. They then moved to Moravia where, under the leadership of Jakob Hutter, they laid the foundations of an Anabaptist community that was to survive in spite of Hutter's own execution in 1536. The *Bruderhof*, as they became known, was an experiment in communal living based on what was believed to be the lives of the early Christians as recorded in the Acts of the Apostles, pacifistic rather than violent, socialistic in their style of living. They eventually found a refuge in 1878–9 in Canada and South Dakota.

Another reformed sect of similar propensities, the Mennonites, taking their name from Menno Simons, a Dutch Anabaptist who had died in 1516, also demonstrated their preference for communal living and religious exclusivity. Their tradition has been maintained in the puritanical rigour and exemplary industry of the Amish Mennonites in modern Pennsylvania.

Very different in character, more alarming and violent, was the radical religious experiment that was set in motion in Münster in 1534. There, a former Lutheran pastor, Berni Rothmann, preached the imminence of the Second Coming of Christ, the necessity for adult baptism and the holding of goods in common. For a time the civic leaders were persuaded to support him while his inflamed teaching drew others of like mind to the city, among them a Dutch Anabaptist, Jan Matthys of Haarlem, who replaced Rothmann as leader. Matthys urged his followers to take up the sword against the ungodly. A fellow Anabaptist leader, the unbalanced but charismatic Jan Beukelsz or Jan of Leyden, declared that no books were permissible save the Bible. He advocated a form of communism that included even the womenfolk. He himself took two wives, one of whom he subsequently had executed. Ordering the expulsion of all Lutherans and Catholics from the city, Jan of Leyden proclaimed himself a messianic king as the successor of King David who would inaugurate the new Jerusalem. Such a subversive religious and social revolution alerted the forces of law and order who, in the shape of the troops of the Bishop of Münster, blockaded and captured the city. Jan of Leyden was taken in chains to be displayed to the public like a performing animal before being tortured and executed with his associate, Bernard Knipperdolling, in January 1536.

The affair at Münster was the only occasion when religious anarchism had a momentary triumph. An Anabaptist from Münster, John of Geelen, a former soldier, did indeed make some forays in the Netherlands marching with his men and women followers through Amsterdam stark naked shouting 'Woe! Woe! The wrath of god falls on this city!' On 10 May 1535 he entered Amsterdam, attacking the city hall during a banquet and killing the burgomaster and several citizens. But for the most part the Anabaptist groups that continued to survive were pacifistic, self-sufficient communities, industrious and highly moral.

There were a few individual dissenters, theologically and usually politically on the left, who acquired a following. Of these the best known was Fausto Sozzini (Socinus), the nephew of an influential Italian scholar from Siena, Fausto's own home town, who had become a Protestant. In 1562 Sozzini wrote a work on St John's Gospel that challenged the divinity of Christ and the immortality of the soul. Settling at Basle, he criticized the evangelical teaching of the reformers and then moved on in 1580 to Poland, where he was to live until his death in 1604, continuing to hold anti-Trinitarian views. He settled on an estate owned by an Anabaptist, Jan Sieninski, that had attracted other Polish radicals who were members of a body known as the Minor Reformed Church of Poland. Although Sozzini was at first refused admission because he was unwilling to be re-baptized, he became identified with the community at Rakow, which he hoped would be the basis of the new Jerusalem. A confession of faith was drawn up in 1605 but the forces of the Counter-Reformation were to bring the Rakow Community to an end. The Jesuits secured the college's closure in 1638 and twenty years later the Socinians were expelled from Poland. Socinus, who attracted a following among individual scholars and intellectuals throughout Europe, was regarded as one of the founding fathers of Unitarianism.

The Protestant Underground which was to flower under the English Commonwealth had only a limited following but that it had come into existence at all was an indication of the religious diversification to which the Reformation gave rise.

Although sectarianism was a feature of the Christian Church from its earliest days, the Reformation, with its stress on the guidance of the individual by the Scriptures, provided a fillip to the propagation of sects that to some degree owed their existence to the Reformation. In the twentieth century, though worldwide in their manifestation, they have found their principle location in America, among them the fast-growing Pentecostalist Church, and in Africa, where Black churches have sometimes provided obscure but colourful progeny, occasionally very bizarre in their nature, which would surely have horrified Luther and Calvin. In some sense by emphasizing reliance on the Scriptures, the Reformation had opened a floodgate that early reformers could not have foreseen.

EIGHT

The Reformation & Society

The Reformation made a revolutionary impact on European society, for the Christian Church, fragmented some 500 or so years earlier by the breakaway of the Eastern Orthodox Church, then suffered an irretrievable fracture. Such fragmentation took place, however, within a framework of orthodox doctrine, the basic foundations of which were accepted by both Protestants and Catholics alike. The nature of God, the sovereign creator of the universe, the sinfulness of man and the redemptive sacrifice of Christ were unchallenged, for the Reformation was essentially a religious movement designed to enhance belief, not to criticize or attack it. What was in question was what constituted right belief.

Yet some at least of the stanchions on which orthodox belief rested had been kicked away. The Pope was no longer accepted by all Christians as the Vicar of Christ, for Protestant cartoonists and writers were to depict him as Anti-Christ. But it was not only the Pope who had been tossed on to the midden. The mediatorial function of the priest had been challenged, since he was no longer recognized as the confessor of the faithful nor did he by his performance of the Mass bring the body and blood of Christ to his earthly flock. Gone too were many of the props that the Church had in the past provided for believers against the insecurity of existence. It was no longer possible to invoke the mediatorial assistance of the Blessed Virgin Mary and the saints. Gone too were the prayers for the dead by which it had seemed possible to assuage the pains of Purgatory for the departed. The worshipper had no treasury of merit laid up in Heaven on which to draw. He was now in some sense responsible for his own salvation, dependent upon his own faith and the authority of Scripture. In this sense at least the Reformation may also be seen as a landmark in the recognition of the individual.

The furnishing of churches converted to Protestant use underlined this break with the past. The figures on the rood screen had been taken away and the screen itself was often removed. Stone altars were smashed and replaced by wooden tables. Holy water stoups had been emptied. Coloured pictures on the walls had been defaced or whitewashed over. Such new churches as were built were more like meeting-houses with the worshipper's attention above all focused on the pulpit and the Bible rather than on the altar. Where the Cross was retained, it replaced the Crucifix, so signifying the Resurrection. The Calvinists had no use for organs. Vestments and altar cloths were packed away and replaced by the Geneva gown; even the surplice was viewed with misgiving and disapproval.

The Reformation did not merely affect the nature of religious belief and practice, in some respects it changed the nature of society. Society, of course, remained a hierarchical order divided into social classes that were deployed into power structures. Yet the Reformation had introduced some new elements into the social scheme. The new Protestant clergy might seem to take the place of their Catholic counterparts; for 'new presbyter was but old priest writ large'. In fact, the ministers of the reformed congregations formed a new and influential professional class. Drawn largely from the urban middle class, they were generally well-educated graduates of universities or trained at the special academies that sprang up in Protestant countries during the sixteenth century to fulfil this task. They were conscientious in seeking to instruct their often ignorant parishioners through the media of their sermons and catechisms, which were issued in large numbers and ideally had to be committed to memory. Many of them complained plaintively of how their parishioners failed to live up to the standards of duty that they set.

This professional clerical class consisted of married men with families. Except for a minority, celibacy had never been a very sensible or possible ideal; and the priest's concubine was a familiar feature of the medieval world. But the clerical family now became a part of the new order, in some instances founding what may be described as clerical dynasties.

There seems to have been no radical distinction between Catholic and Protestant family values. Both required fidelity in marriage and disapproved of divorce and condemned all sexual deviations: it was taken for granted that wives should be subordinate to their husbands and children to their parents. Although the Counter-Reformation also tended to regurgitate a set of puritanical values, Protestant society, especially where Calvinism was dominant, sought to impose an austere moral code. Grace at meals and family prayers became normal while the sabbatarianism which particularly gripped England and Scotland and which became a characteristic feature of religion in New England in America was very much a child of the Reformation. The Puritan ethic was expressed through disapproval of the theatre and forms of artistic licence, attendance at balls and in playing cards and dice, as well as in the condemnation of undue luxury in dress and behaviour and in a strong abhorrence of swearing or any form of bawdiness or indecency.

Women played a significant part in furthering the Reformation, acting as patrons and protectors, especially if they were noble gentlewomen of reforming ideas. While the Reformers never envisaged a female ministry, the Reformation, by desacralizing the priesthood, opened a chink that, three centuries later, would make it possible for Protestant denominations to accept a female ministry.

Much has been made, perhaps too much, of the Protestant work ethic that was associated by some writers, notably Max Weber in Germany and R.H. Tawney in England, with the rise of capitalistic society. It would be difficult to prove that Protestantism was explicitly responsible for the expansion of capitalism so characteristic of the post-Reformation world. Catholics were as much to the fore as Protestants in generating the capitalistic industrial society. Yet the emphasis that the Reformers placed on man's calling, his vocation which Luther termed *Die Beruf*, helped to create the work ethic, with its emphasis on thrift and condemnation of idleness; certainly it promoted the effective fulfilment of secular tasks in everyday work and appeared to justify the material success that this brought about. If it is not an argument that can be pushed too far, Protestantism may yet have been an ingredient in the rise of the successful business, some of whose leading beneficiaries, especially in the United States, were themselves to be generous benefactors to the Reformed Churches.

Protestantism did not adumbrate any particular form of government, save that it should be godly. But whereas Catholicism appeared more likely to favour or at least to acquiesce in an authoritarian form of government, Protestantism, with its notion of the brotherhood of believers, was more sympathetic to democratic forms of government. Confronted with the dilemma of a Christian's duty to an ungodly or tyrannical ruler, it would, as the Religious Wars in France showed, even justify popular rebellion. Although the issues in the English Civil War are too complex and confused to allow a final judgement as to what brought it into being, Cromwell and his fellow Puritans would have argued that they were fighting against an unjust king on behalf of God's people; the period of the Commonwealth witnessed the generation of an extraordinary welter of religious groups that were in essence democratic in their objectives. It is certainly arguable that in the long run the Reformation was a step on the road to democratic government.

The European Reformation was a positive movement, acting as a spur to the Counter-Reformation that, partly through the work of the Jesuits and the Council of Trent, was to reshape the Catholic Church and endow it with new vitality. The Reformation had opened up a treasury of spiritual resources, making available a fountain of spirituality, especially through the medium of the open Bible, for, as William Chillingworth observed in 1638, 'the Bible only I say is the religion of Protestants'. It had created a new awareness of man's relationship with God, virtually placing in practice the responsibility for man's salvation with man himself. It had helped to bring about a changed society and inspired a missionary impulse so that its shock-waves, if perhaps with the passage of time showing signs of weakening, long continued to be felt in all parts of the world.

With the passage of time the way in which historians have interpreted the Reformation has changed. In earlier history, religious prejudice gave rise to some distorted history; for Protestants, the Reformation was seen primarily as a movement of religious change in a progressive direction, and by their critics as the phenomenon that fractured the unity of the Christian Church. But historians have become increasingly aware of its inner complexities and its secular impulses. Even the bitterness and strife to which for centuries it gave rise have been mollified, so that by 1998 it seemed likely that the Roman Church and Lutheran World Federation were on the brink of reaching a doctrinal consensus which admitted that both faith and good works, granted by the grace of God, were equally important in the work of man's salvation. By the close of the twentieth century the Reformation appeared less as a solely religious movement than as an amalgam of interactive social and political as well as religious aspirations at work in a historical context, the development of which had been profoundly shaped by the events that took place in sixteenth-century Europe.

Further Reading

GENERAL

Cameron, E. *The European Reformation*, Oxford, 1991, a good comprehensive survey.

Chadwick, Owen. *The Reformation*, Harmondsworth, 1964, a well-balanced introduction.

Cheanu, P. (ed.). *The Reformation*, Gloucester, 1989, some valuable essays.

Elton, Geoffrey (ed.). *The Reformation, 1520–59*, 2nd edn, 1990.

McGrath, A.E. *Reformation Thought*, 2nd edn, Oxford, 1993, a theological approach.

Spitz, L.W. *The Protestant Reformation*, New York, 1986, a useful discussion.

LUTHER AND THE GERMAN REFORMATION

Bainton, R. *Here I Stand; a Life of Martin Luther*, London, 1955, a much acclaimed biography.

Bornkamm, H. *Luther's World of Thought*, London, 1958, explores the intellectual background.

Dickens, A.G. *The German Nation and Martin Luther*, London, 1974, a fine study of the relationship between Martin Luther and the German people.

Fife, R.H. *The Revolt of Martin Luther*, New York, 1957, a detailed examination of the beginnings of the German Reformation.

Obermann, H. *Luther: Man, God and the Devil*, London, 1989, an authoritative examination of Luther's theology.

Rupp, E.G. *Patterns of Reformation*, London, 1969.

Scribner, R.W. *The German Reformation*, London, 1986, a good general survey.

Strauss, Gerald. *Luther's House of Learning: Indoctrination of the Young in the German Reformation*, New York, 1978, throws light on the relationship between Protestant education and the social and political structure.

FURTHER READING

ZWINGLI

Potter, G.R. *Zwingli*, Cambridge, 1976.
Stephens, W.P. *The Theology of Huldrych Zwingli*, Oxford, 1986.

THE REFORMATION IN SCANDINAVIA

Grill, O.P. (ed.). *The Scandinavian Reformation*, Cambridge, 1995, useful essays.

THE ENGLISH REFORMATION

Brigden, Susan, *London and the Reformation*, Oxford, 1989, an original and valuable account of the course of the Reformation in London.
Collinson, P. *The Birthpangs of Protestant England*, London, 1988.
——. *The Religion of Protestants: the Church in English Society*, Oxford, 1982.
——. *The Elizabethan Puritan Movement*, London, 1967.
All illuminating works by an acknowledged expert.
Daniell, D. *William Tyndale*, New Haven, Conn., 1994, a valuable biography.
Dickens, A.G. *The English Reformation*, London, 1964, still the best general survey.
Duffy, E.A. *The Stripping of the Altars*, New Haven, Conn., 1992, an interesting work of original research, throwing light on the character and range of late medieval Catholicism.
Haigh, Christopher (ed.). *The English Reformation Revised*, Cambridge, 1987, queries some of the accepted interpretations.
MacCulloch, D. *Thomas Cranmer*, New Haven, Conn., 1996, an outstanding biography.
Scarisbrick, J.J. *The Reformation and the English People*, Oxford, 1984.

CALVIN

Hopfl, H. *The Christian Polity of John Calvin*, London, 1982, discusses Calvin's political thought.
McGrath, A.E. *John Calvin*, Oxford, 1990, a balanced biography.
McNeill, J.T. *The History and Character of Calvinism*, New York, rev. edn, 1967, a reliable general survey.
Parker, T.H.L. *Calvin*, London, 1975.

Pettegree, A., Duke, A. and Lewis, G. *Calvinism in Europe*, 1994.
Prestwich, M. (ed.). *International Calvinism, 1541–1725*, Oxford, 1985, a series of informative essays.

THE SCOTTISH REFORMATION

Cowen, I.B. *The Scottish Reformation*, New York, 1982.
Donaldson, G. *The Scottish Reformation*, Cambridge, 1960, a good general survey.
Wormald, J. *Court, Kirk and Community, Scotland 1470–1625*, London, 1981, explores the relationship between religious change and society.

THE FRENCH REFORMATION

Davis, Natalie Z. *Society and Culture in Early Modern France*, London, 1961.
Greengrass, Mark. *The French Reformation*, London, 1987, a useful general survey.

THE REFORMATION IN THE LOW COUNTRIES

Crew, P.M. *Calvinist Preaching and Iconoclasm in the Netherlands, 1544–69*, Cambridge, 1978.
Duke, A. *Reformation and Revolt in the Netherlands*, London, 1990, a valuable survey.
Parker, G. *The Dutch Revolt*, London, 1977, a general history that explores the relationship between politics and religion.

THE PROTESTANT UNDERGROUND

Clasen, C.P. *Anabaptism: A Social History*, London, 1972.
Estep, W. *The Anabaptist Story*, 3rd edn, Grand Rapids, Michigan, 1996.
Scott, T. *Thomas Müntzer: Theology and Revolution in the German Reformation*, London, 1989.
Williams, G.H. *The Radical Reformation*, 3rd edn, London, 1992, a useful, comprehensive survey.

Index

Bold type indicates main or more significant entries.